About the Title
Happiness in the Family

Choice Theory defines all behavior as being total behavior and states that it is designated by verbs, usually infinitives and gerunds, and named by the component that is most recognizable. Therefore, *happiness* is the choice of being happy and *angering* is the choice of acting out in anger. Within the family these take many forms from the highs of happiness to the lows of rage and aggression between family members—father and mother, parent and child, or between siblings.

This book discusses the various forms of angering that are found within the family and alternate ways to cope with and reduce the angering to bring about calmness and happiness for the members of the family. Frustrations are a result of differences between the world, as we perceive it and the world as we would like it. This discussion on angering includes an expanded writing on the subject of Choice Theory that can bring true happiness within the family.

Additional information given relates to dealing with parenting, stress, and angering and its management to bring about a state of calm in the family that was never thought possible. Much of the anxiety and frustration in the family is brought about by events in the community and the family's interaction within the community. Suggestions as to proposed actions by individuals in the public, community as a whole, state, and nation to angering and aggression are given.

Endorsements

Dr. J. Thomas Bellows states in *Happiness in the Family—Using Choice Theory to Eliminate Hostility in the Family* that, "My primary responsibility as a facilitator of domestic violence, family aggression, and parenting groups is to create a satisfying relationship with my clients and from this relationship, to teach them to find increasingly healthier ways to relate to others in their lives." The theory, applications and stories he shares create a relationship of caring, concern and reality with the reader. *Happiness in the Family*, with its blend of Choice Theory, domestic violence, and parenting information, accomplishes Dr. Bellows' goals.

—Robert G. Hoglund
President and founder of Bob Hoglund, Inc.
Tempe, Arizona
Author: *The School for Quality Learning*
Intervention Strategies
Educating for Responsibility and Quality™
Numerous articles on education and quality management
William Glasser Institute, Senior Faculty
Loyola Marymount University, Faculty Member

Unbridled anger can drive a wedge into what we want and need most in our relationships—love and belonging. Dr. Bellows shows us how to win against the anger trap which is only one small "d" away from danger. Our prisons are filled with those who lost the battle. I have learned a great deal from my review of *Happiness in the Family—Using Choice Theory to Eliminate Hostility in the Family* and it has my strong recommendation. Dr. Bellows has done a masterful job in showing how Choice Theory works in the most difficult situations.

—LuNel LeMieux
Community Circle Coordinator
The Maple Counseling Center
Beverly Hills, California

Verbal abuse, covert harassment, bullying and violence are secretive and paralyzing behaviors that affect families, relationships and trust. The uncertainty that comes with experiencing intermittent emotional misbehavior leaves people feeling alone and frightened. *Happiness in the family—Using Choice Theory to Eliminate Hostility in the Family* continues what Dr. J. Thomas Bellows started in his first book, *Angering in the Family*. Dr. Bellows gives helpful information and tools to transform helplessness to hopefulness. Dr. Bellows speaks openly and practically about the need for awareness, prevention, family intervention and collaboration. Dr. Bellows' application of Dr. William Glasser's Choice Theory and Reality Therapy techniques to family violence and his explanations of how anger harms people's lives are valuable to both professionals and lay people. Individuals can learn ways that intimidating partners and family members can receive treatment. They will realize they are not alone. Families can avail themselves of information for treatment that forms new and positive connections. Abusers will benefit from Dr. Bellows' information but most of all they will learn techniques that give hope for change.

—**Brandi Roth, Ph.D.**
  Psychologist, Consultant and Educator in Beverly Hills, California
  Faculty member of The William Glasser Institute
  Reality Therapy Certified
  Basic Week Phase II Instructor Training
  Co-author: *Secrets to School Success*
                      Relationship Counseling with Choice Theory Strategies
                      Role Play Handbook, Understanding and Teaching the New Reality Therapy
                      Counseling with Choice Theory Through Role Play

Dr. J. Thomas Bellows openly addresses that which many shy away from or choose not to talk about. He is a champion in his field as he guides those in need (and those not addressing the fact that they have a need) to take the steps to choose positive behaviors. Dr. Bellows firsthand stories and professional experience bring anger and relationships to light as well as the many difficult behaviors affecting daily life. *Happiness in the Family—Using Choice Theory to Eliminate Hostility in the Family* is comprised of Dr. Bellows' notes, stories, advice and insight so readers can find the message and meaning that relates to them personally. Readers will identify with the words and patterns, making discoveries as they read *Happiness in the Family*. Dr. Bellows' guides his audience to find/ appreciate that sometimes it is the little things coming to the surface that bring relevant choices and change. This reader friendly book is a true masterpiece to help readers master a difference in their lives and those around them.

> —**Gail Endelman Small**
> Fulbright Memorial Scholar
> People to People Ambassador
> Author: *Joyful Learning-No One Ever Wants to Go to Recess!*
> *Joyful Parenting-Before You Blink They'll be Grown*
> *The Spelling Bee and Me-A Real-Life Adventure in Learning*
> *The Big Squeal-A Wild, True, and Twisted Tail*
> *Life's Little Lessons-An Inch-by-Inch Tale of Success*
> International Inspirational Speaker and Educational Consultant
> Who's Who among America's Teachers 2005 and 2006
> Reality Therapy Certified

Happiness in the Family

Happiness in the Family

Using Choice Theory to Eliminate
Hostility in the Family

J. Thomas Bellows, Ph.D.

iUniverse, Inc.
New York   Lincoln   Shanghai

Happiness in the Family
Using Choice Theory to Eliminate Hostility in the Family

iUniverse books may be ordered through booksellers or by contacting:

iUniverse
2021 Pine Lake Road, Suite 100
Lincoln, NE 68512
www.iuniverse.com
1-800-Authors (1-800-288-4677)

Because of the dynamic nature of the Internet, any Web addresses or links contained in this book may have changed since publication and may no longer be valid.

The views expressed in this work are solely those of the author and do not necessarily reflect the views of the publisher, and the publisher hereby disclaims any responsibility for them.

Author's photograph taken by David Gomez of David Gomez Photography.

ISBN: 978-0-595-43129-8 (pbk)
ISBN: 978-0-595-87474-3 (ebk)

Printed in the United States of America

I wish to dedicate this book to my wife, Jill, and to my sons, John and Colin. Additionally, I would like to dedicate this book to the William Glasser Institute members who practice and promote Choice Theory.

Contents

PART I: CHOICE THEORY AND ANGERING

Acknowledgments

I acknowledge my family and the information they provided for me to use in my self-evaluation and the acceptance of Choice Theory as my intended way of life. They gave me support and assistance while I was writing this book. Without their caring behavior, this book never would have come into being.

I would also like to acknowledge all of my clients who have shared themselves with me in an effort to reduce the angering in their families and in the community, especially those who graciously allowed me to share their stories to illustrate some of the points in this book. These people have given of themselves in an effort to learn Choice Theory and apply it to their lives and the lives of their families. We have shared tears and laughter along with the serious discussions on how to live a violence-free life.

I wish to thank William Glasser, M.D., Carleen Glasser, M.A., Brandi Roth, Ph.D., and the other faculty of the William Glasser Institute and the Choice Theory community. They gave of their valuable time to help me learn Reality Therapy and Choice Theory and their participation in role-playing gave me experience in using what I learned with my domestic violence or family aggression clients.

Finally, I acknowledge the community in which I live, Los Angeles, for exposing me to many of the issues that are discussed here, and the situations that led me to the conclusions at which I have arrived.

Foreword

Dr. J. Thomas Bellows, a very valuable member of the William Glasser Institute, has written a revised edition of a previous book, *Angering in the Family*. *Happiness in the Family—Using Choice Theory to Eliminate Hostility in the Family*, is a book you can not only read yourself, but can share with the individuals and the unhappy families with whom you work. To me, the most usable concept in the book, a concept that Tom and I have often discussed, is **external control psychology** or, put more simply, **external control**.

For the foreseeable future, all of us will continue to live in a world completely dominated by external control. There are about six thousand societies in our world and every one of these societies, large and small, rich or poor, religious or not, and regardless of skin color, employ external control whenever its members have difficulty getting along with each other. When they use external control, it harms or destroys every relationship in which it is used. Yet, for all practical purposes, external control has penetrated our thinking to the point it has become common sense.

What makes the external control way of relating to each other so deadly is that the people who use it firmly believe that it is the right thing to do. For example, in the United States, half of the marriages end in divorce and almost all of these are caused by external control by one partner over the other or the fight for supremacy of control between the two parties. All of this family misery, including violence and even murder, is the result of one or both members of the marriage firmly believing that there is no viable alternative to using external control on each other.

What I believe, and Tom explains clearly in *Happiness in the Family*, is that there is a pleasant alternative to external control. I have labeled it **Choice Theory.** Choice Theory is both easy and enjoyable to learn. While adding this concept to your counseling repertoire takes a little effort, its effect is dramatically positive. I know this statement may seem excessive, but as you read this book and teach the concepts to the people with whom you work, you will be rewarded by a great deal of heads nodding in agreement as their minds begin to absorb what to most of them is a very new idea.

—**William Glasser, M.D.**
> Creator of Choice Theory®, Reality Therapy, Quality School Program, and Lead-Management
> Author of many books and articles on the application of his theories
> President of the William Glasser Institute

Preface

Behavior is necessary to bring about a state of happiness within an individual and calmness in a family. *Happiness in the Family—Using Choice Theory to Eliminate Hostility in the Family* relates to the behavior that reduces the hostility and brings calmness and happiness back to the family. After publishing *Angering in the Family*, a great deal of additional information came to my attention so that I thought it necessary to add to the original concept. In doing so, the focus of the book has changed from angering to bringing happiness to an angering family.

Dr. Glasser defines happiness as:

> *"Enjoying the life you are choosing to live, getting along well with the people near and dear to you, doing something with your life you believe is worthwhile, and not doing anything to deprive anyone else of the same chance for the happiness you have."* (Glasser, 1998)

Emotions are caused by thinking, acting, feeling, and physiology which are the elements of total behavior. There are six basic emotions-anger, disgust, fear, sadness, surprise, and happiness. Ranked from anger to happiness, they either push people apart or draw people together. The actions that push people apart are called the deadly habits and the actions that draw people together are called the caring habits. These habits are the response to the ultimate question—If I say or do __(blank)__ will it bring us closer together or will it push us farther apart? Obviously we want to bring our loved ones closer together instead of pushing them farther apart from us. Therefore, we will want to do the caring habits instead of the deadly habits to bring happiness into the family.

I have included a chapter on ways the community can support a family, in addition to much material on how the members of the family can change themselves to caring people and thus create a caring and calm family. In addition, throughout *Happiness in the Family* I have addressed this community perspective and the happiness that can be obtained within the family as a result of dealing with the angering that brings tension and unhappiness. I have also better explained and exemplified some of the elements of Choice Theory to assist readers in applying its concepts to themselves and their families to bring about a state of happiness that they have never achieved in the past. I have reused some of the stories that appeared in *Angering in the Family* because they illustrate the points that need to be made in this book. All of the stories actually occurred in my counseling sessions and are not made up for illustrative purposes.

PART I

CHOICE THEORY AND ANGERING

CHAPTER 1

Introduction

This book is the result of more than a decade of counseling angering families, aggressive domestic partners, or domestic violence batterers; investigating child abuse allegations; and attending conferences and other training sessions dealing with violence in the family. These experiences have taught me that it is the person—his or her individual choices—that is responsible for the aggressive acts, not the other person's actions or life circumstances. *The responsibility lies solely with the aggressor.* These experiences have led me to believe that Reality Therapy with Choice Theory is a viable therapeutic model for counseling aggressive clients. When a client becomes less angering and calmer, then the family can move toward calmness as a unit.

The purpose of this book is to demonstrate and explain a more appropriate method of relating to family members (spouse, mate, child, and other significant persons) in one's life that can bring happiness to all family members. Communication difficulties are worsened when one individual insists he or she is right and the other is wrong or that one partner has the right to make the decisions for the family without regard to the wishes of the other family members. Choice Theory teaches that the problem with which one struggles is usually not a simple issue of right and wrong. Oh, how nice it would be if all of the choices in life were black or white, right or wrong!

The use of Reality Therapy with Choice Theory applied to a family that consists of father, mother and his/hers/theirs child(ren) is illustrated by Lute and his wife Terri and his son by a different woman, her daughter by a different man and their daughter. The description of Lute's and Terri's life together is given in Appendix A. This type of blended family is becoming more prevalent and the anger and frustration as a result of the failed relationships is being dealt with by the courts and the community. This may appear to be a composite family, but in actuality it is one blended family. Lute attended my domestic violence groups. Terri attended my parenting classes and I monitored the visits between the children and their fathers. This book addresses some of the problems that such a family may have and a means to overcome the ongoing relationship problems. The methods and information discussed within this book are used in domestic violence groups to satisfy court ordered counseling and to assist the primary aggressor to learn to deal with the frustrations of life and in a relationship. They are also used in the parenting classes to help the parents bring about calmness between them and their children and how to raise children using Choice Theory. The court does not often require the entire family to attend counseling to address the angering and inappropriate parenting in the family.

This example relates both Lute's and Terri's, version of their life together. Lute's version differs from Terri's. The reader can see the manner in which Lute makes himself out to be a hero to the other members of a domestic violence group and Terri makes him out to be the villain and justifies her decision to stay away from him. Terri received counseling from her sheltered residence before moving back into the community and parenting classes after leaving the shelter. Each person's perception comes from the view point of the person telling the story and may be different from what an unrelated third party may have experienced and reported. What real world version would a camera have reported?

Members of Lute's group give their unedited version of the events in their life. With one-sided groups, the facilitator has to retain the perspective that the reports made by the group member are their perceptions and not necessarily an accurate representation of what happened in real world. It is very difficult for an aggressive and controlling person to confess in front of fifteen other men that he beat or abused a woman. It is also difficult for a parent to admit they do not know how to deal with a child or what they learned from their parents is not correct. The offender knows what he or she did, but finds it difficult to admit it in public. Angering in the family in the form of aggressive acts against a mate and/or children is most often behind closed doors and not discussed in public.

Often the reported versions change with time because the member becomes more at ease with the group and himself. When this occurs, the member may be more willing to acknowledge just how aggressive he was and what kind of physical and emotional abuse to which he may have subjected his partner or his children. Only then can true change occur in an aggressor's life.

The fear that the anger will return is one of the lasting trust issues that couples with aggression have. Like an addict's relapse, the return of aggression can destroy the relationship again, possibly this time with greater or more permanent results. The angry person may have confidence in his or her ability to remain violence-free, but the loved one is always on the watch for the tell-tale signs of the return of the violent behavior. Continued use of caring behavior and a demonstration of a high commitment to nonviolence are the primary methods that the aggressor can use to develop a high level of trust between him and his partner.

This family situation sets the stage for the group counseling sessions in which I have been using Choice Theory and Reality Therapy. Could there be improvements over this method of domestic violence counseling? The laws in California make mandatory court-sanctioned therapeutic intervention impossible for both parties of the violent relationship. Until a series of joint sessions is accepted by the courts in domestic violence cases, we are subjected to a one-sided approach. Joint counseling should occur after the aggressor(s) has learned to deal with frustration without violence. Other states and countries have allowed joint family counseling with success.

I have noticed a real change in some of the clients, but have no way of establishing the true picture of family life in a home where the two parties continue to live with each other after the completion of the court-ordered sessions. The family above is unique because I have had an ongoing dialogue with both parties.

Many of the clients separate from the partners in the incident and it is unknown if either of them continue their behavior after completing the court-ordered punishment. The spouses are encouraged to stay in contact with the agency that provides counseling to the aggressor, but they seldom report their side of the events. Most of them do not even participate in the free counseling that is provided by the state. Many of them state that they believe that since the aggressor was found guilty, he was at fault; since they are the victims, they have done nothing wrong. Therefore, the victim continues to behave in the same fashion as when they were being abused. This often leads to either continued abuse by the partner from the incident or by a new partner.

Lute and Terri set the stage for the counseling addressed in this book. Their story illustrates how families that are dysfunctional in one area are often dysfunctional in many areas. Families such as Lute and Terri's just don't have one problem; they have many at the same time.

In his book, *Choice Theory, A New Psychology of Personal Freedom* (1998), Dr. Glasser states that in an abusive family, the perpetrator is following the most destructive external control practice: the abuser believes he or she owns the partner and children. And to a great extent, the legal system of the external-control society we live in supports that belief. Men can beat, abuse, rape, or exploit their wives and children and get away with it because the men who run our present society are, for the most part, afraid they will lose power if wives are legitimately protected by the law. This acceptance of spousal and child brutality needs to be changed, and teaching Choice Theory to all people, including abusers, has proven to reduce the recidivism rate of perpetrators, Rachor (1995).

Women and children are not chattel. No one has the right to beat anyone, and people who are beaten need legal protection. The victim's testimony is not needed to convict a batterer if there is other evidence to substantiate the crime, but this law is under review by the Supreme Court as it is in conflict with the Sixth Amendment to the U.S. Constitution that contains the clause allowing the accused "to be confronted with the witnesses against him." Even if the perpetrator is sentenced, punishing him or her does little good if that is all that happens, because is the government is merely using control to punish control. When perpetrators are court-ordered to my groups, they are taught Choice Theory and Reality Therapy in a group setting with others who have the same domestic violence or parenting problem. The court orders the perpetrator to attend, but makes counseling for the victim voluntary.

Why is managing the choice to anger (angering) so difficult? Angering is experienced more frequently than other emotions. Angering is as intense as fear and includes high sympathetic nervous system arousal. Angering lasts longer than other emotional states. Angering produces a strong tendency to approach, rather than avoid, the person or situation toward which the anger is directed. Instead of separating from that which is unpleasant, as would happen in other unpleasant situations, angering draws those in conflict together and may cause the situation to escalate into aggressive acts between the parties. Angering induces an experience of greater power or potency than do the other emotions. Angering can be addictive because it produces adrenalin, a mood-altering and addictive chemical. Happiness is the only emotion people are less likely to want to change than angering.

I want to illustrate that it is not the other person or external event that causes the perpetrators to be calm or to be angry. Rather, it is their *total behavior* (how they think, act, feel, and their body physiology) regarding the person or event which leads to the choice of actions. Angering has many negative consequences because all of our total behavior is measured in the real world. Angering often leads to verbal and physical aggression and decreased problem solving. Calm or non-angering total behavior leads to assertiveness and increased problem solving. Clients gain much happiness when they examine their choices to anger and replace the beliefs which make it acceptable with choices of calmness. They learn that calmness will bring them together with others instead of driving them away.

It is not life's circumstances that make you angry. It is how you choose to behave about that circumstance that leads to your choice to act upon your anger.

Dr. Glasser (1998) describes a Quality Community in Chapter Twelve of his book, *Choice Theory, A New Psychology of Personal Freedom.* His description lists the people that he believes need to be involved in starting such a community. He lists politicians, business and labor administrators, media personnel, religious leaders, judges, charitable institutions, educational leaders, medical and counseling workers, police and fire departments, interested citizens of the community, women's groups, civil rights groups, and service clubs. He states that when these people work together to bring the citizens of the community closer together instead of driving them farther apart, violence, aggression, and hostility will be reduced and happiness and mental health can be achieved for most of the residents.

Dr. Glasser (2005) gives the following definition of mental health.

You are mentally healthy if you enjoy being with most of the people you know, especially with the important people in your life such as family, sexual partners, and friends. Generally, you are happy and are more than willing to help an unhappy family member, friend, or colleague to feel better. You lead a mostly tension-free life, laugh a lot, and rarely suffer from the aches and pains that so many people accept as an unavoidable part of living. You enjoy life and have no trouble accepting other people who think and act differently from you. It rarely occurs to you to criticize or try to change anyone. If you have differences with someone else you will try to work out the problem; if you can't you will walk away before you argue and increase the difficulty.

You are creative in what you attempt and may enjoy more of your potential than you ever thought possible. Finally, even in very difficult situations when you are unhappy—no one can be happy all the time—you'll know why you are unhappy and attempt to do something about it. You may even be physically handicapped as was Christopher Reeve, and still fit the criteria above.

Tal Ben-Shahar at Harvard University teaches about happiness in his Psychology 1504 course, Positive Psychology. He gives six tips for happiness that correlate with Choice Theory as described by Dr. Glasser. The tips and their description using the language of Choice Theory follow.

1. **Give yourself permission to be human.**
    Feelings, such as anger, fear, sadness, or anxiety, are natural and something we do not have direct control over. We are more likely to overcome them when we accept them as natural. Rejecting these feelings as, positive or negative, is like rejecting ourselves and leads to frustration and unhappiness.

2. **Happiness lies at the intersection between pleasure and meaning.**
    Our total behavior at work or at home should be both personally significant and enjoyable. When this is not feasible, make sure we have happiness boosters, moments throughout the week that provide us with both pleasure and meaning.

3. **Keep in mind that happiness is mostly dependent on your state of mind, not on your status or the state of your bank account.**

    In all but the most extreme circumstances, our level of well being is determined by what we choose to focus on and by our interpretation or perception of the external events of the real world. For example, do we perceive failure as disastrous and a reflection on our inabilities, or do we see it as a learning opportunity?

4. **Simplify!**

    Are we, generally, too busy, trying to accomplish more activities in less time? When we try to do more, we may sacrifice the quality of the work we do. All of our total behavior is designed to satisfy one or more of our basic needs, so totally behaving with quality actions and thoughts bring more happiness into our life.

5. **Remember the mind-body connection.**

    The mind is influenced by the actions of the body. Total behavior consists of the two directly controllable elements, actions and thoughts, and the two indirectly controllable elements, feelings and physiology. Regular exercise, adequate sleep, and healthy eating habits lead to both physical and mental health.

6. **Express gratitude whenever possible.**

    Are you taking your life for granted? Learn to be grateful for and relish the magnificent things in life, from friends to fun activities, from environment to a pleasant face.

All people deserve to use the tips Professor Ben-Shahar gives to have the mental health and happiness that Dr. Glasser defines.

CHAPTER 2

Choice Theory and Hostility

Some Basics of Choice Theory

Choice Theory is the basis for all programs taught by the William Glasser Institute. It states that all we do is behave, that almost all behavior is chosen, and that we are driven by our genes to satisfy the fundamentals of human motivation—the five basic needs are *survival, love and belonging, power, freedom,* and *fun.* All behavior is described as total behavior and consists of *acting, thinking, feelings,* and *physiology.*

Happiness or mental health is defined as enjoying the life you are choosing to live, getting along well with the people near and dear to you, doing something with your life you believe is worthwhile, and not doing anything to deprive anyone else of the same chance for the happiness that you have. (Glasser, 1998) Reality Therapy is used to help the client gain happiness and move into a state of mental health. Choice Theory is a way of living that illustrates how clients can use caring habits instead of deadly habits to live in harmony with the other members of their families.

The caring habits are *supporting, encouraging, listening, accepting, trusting, respecting, and negotiating differences,* and the deadly habits are *criticizing, blaming, complaining, nagging, threatening, punishing, and rewarding to control (bribing).* Additionally, the ultimate question—*Will my action bring me closer to others in the community or will it tend to move us farther apart?*—refers to these habits. If we use the caring habits instead of the deadly habits, and if each person is responsible for their choices and total behaviors, then the objective of the reduction of aggression in the society can be accomplished.

This model is a dramatically different approach for clients who have used anger and violence to gain control of the people around them and force their form of happiness on the family. In group, we discuss solutions to the everyday situations that arise in the members' lives and use the concepts of Choice Theory to arrive at caring behavior that will satisfy the needs of each person in the family.

In practice, the most important need is love and belonging, as closeness and connectedness with the people we care about is a requisite for satisfying all of our needs. Choice Theory replaces external control psychology, the psychology model used by almost all the people in the world.

The ten axioms of Choice Theory follow:

1. *The only person whose behavior we can control is our own.* Control of another person is the crux of the family aggression issue. We are responsible for what we do. If we really accept the idea that we choose our behavior and generate our emotional response, then we will not waste time and energy making excuses.

    Using Choice Theory does not mean we stop caring about others. It means we have an inner wisdom telling us what we can control and what we cannot. When family members are struggling with temptations to return to abusive behaviors, we need to detach. When family members or friends are engaged in the deadly habits, we need to care, but not protect them from the results of their behavior. Sometimes close friends will be off base in the way they talk to us. We practice detachment by not reacting to the person but being responsive to the inner message of what kind of people we wish to be.

    Individuals cannot control another person's behavior. Inner security will never come from how someone else behaves. The most helpful thing we can do for someone is to listen and care; then we need to be ready to let go of the outcome.

2. *Humans are driven by five genetic needs*: survival, love and belonging, power, freedom, and fun. All members of the family have the same basic needs, but each member may have a different level of a specific need and a different total behavior that satisfies the need.

3. *Individuals can satisfy these needs only by satisfying a picture or pictures in their quality worlds.* Of all we know, what we choose to put into our quality worlds is the most important.

4. *All we can do from birth to death is to behave*: acting, thinking, feeling, and physiology.

5. *All total behavior is designated by verbs, usually infinitives and gerunds, and named by the component that is most recognizable.* The symptoms of anxiety, depression, and anger are emotional expressions of the total behavior that we generate. They are a part of a discouraged person's generated response—the attempt to gain a sense of inner control when the real world is perceived as disappointing. The culture of external control tells us to think of these symptoms as conditions over which we have little or no control.

6. *All total behavior is chosen, but we have direct control over only the acting and thinking components.* The generated behavior elements are feeling and physiology. We always choose behavior for the purpose of meeting one or more of the five basic needs. The behavior that satisfies the father's need may not be the same behavior that satisfies the mother's or the children's needs.

7. *All we can give or get from other people is information.* How we deal with that information is our choice. We have control over ourselves only, as the first axiom states, and we cannot control any other person. We have influence over those we come in touch with who are involved directly with our lives. But, we have no control and often little influence over the rest of the people in the world. All that can

pass between people is information—not control. The largest myth in the family is that the parents can control the children. They can teach and influence, but not control. The children will make their own choices based on the information they have at the time.

8. *All long-lasting psychological problems are relationship problems.* The lack of calmness in the family is a result of these relationship problems.

9. *The problem relationship is always part of our present lives.* When the actions of members of the family change, the problem relationships will change and they will be lessened. The family will become calmer.

10. *Painful events from the past have a great deal to do with what we are today, but revisiting this painful past can contribute little or nothing to what we need to do now: improve an important, present relationship.* It is never too late to make the changes that are needed to improve the important, present relationships within the family.

Choice Theory suggests that family members can bring about a positive relationship by using the seven caring habits: *supporting, encouraging, listening, accepting, trusting, respecting,* and *negotiating the differences.* These are differentiated from the seven deadly habits that will bring frustration and anger into the relationship: *criticizing, blaming, complaining, nagging, threatening, punishing,* and *bribing or rewarding to control.*

The chart, "How the Brain Works" (*Chart Talk*), was created by William Glasser as a description of the interactions of the brain and his concept of Choice Theory. I have found that, in group work with domestic violence aggressors and parents, the simplified version of the chart given in Chapter Four of this book can facilitate the use of the clients' own events in place of the description of the theory, thus personalizing the counseling. Each element in the simplified chart can be tailored to the discussion with the client without complicating the therapeutic process.

Frustration

Frustration is the emotion that we experience when we do not get what we think we should or must get, or when we are denied that to which we believe we are entitled. We experience the emotion when we are starkly confronted by the realization that we cannot control others. The emotion of frustration activates the sympathetic nervous system physiology (e.g., increasing heart rate, increasing muscle tension, etc.) and results in a significantly increased likelihood of aggressive behavior accompanied by seriously diminished problem solving and parenting skills and damaged interpersonal relationships. We experience frustration when we do not get what we prefer, desire, hope, want, or wish for. Frustration is the feeling felt when we perceive the world around us to be different from the way we would have the world to be, i.e., our perceived world is different from our quality world. We choose various total behaviors depending on the level and circumstances of our frustration. One of the often made choices is angering.

When we are upset by the actions of others, we need to try to keep in mind that they are not usually trying to hurt us. In most cases they are doing what they think is best to satisfy their needs; they have not even considered how it will affect us. How we choose to respond to that person's actions and lack of consideration is up to us. We have control over what comes next.

Angering

In the most general sense, angering is a total behavior that ranges from mild irritation to intense fury and rage. Angering is a natural response to those situations in which we feel threatened, we believe harm will come to us, or we believe that another person has unnecessarily wronged us. We may also choose angering when we feel another person, such as a child, is being threatened or harmed. This reaction is a result of the biological drive to protect the young for the survival of the species. In addition, angering may result from frustration when our needs, desires, and goals are not being met. When we choose angering, we may lose our patience and act impulsively, aggressively, or violently.

People often confuse angering with aggression. Aggression is an action that is intended to cause harm to another person or damage property. This total behavior can include verbal abuse, threats, or violent acts. Angering, on the other hand, is a total behavior that does not necessarily lead to aggression. Therefore, a person can choose angering without choosing to act aggressively.

A term related to angering and aggression is hostility. Hostility refers to a complex set of attitudes and judgments that motivate aggressive behaviors. Whereas angering is a total behavior and aggression is only an action, hostility is an attitude or belief that involves disliking others and evaluating them negatively.

Anger becomes a problem when it is felt too intensely, is felt too frequently, or is expressed inappropriately. Feeling anger too intensely or frequently places extreme physical strain on the body. During prolonged and frequent episodes of anger, certain divisions of the nervous system become highly activated. Consequently, blood pressure and heart rate increase and stay elevated for long periods. This stress on the body may produce many different health problems such as hypertension, heart disease, and diminished immune system efficiency. Thus, from a health standpoint, avoiding physical illness is a motivation for controlling anger.

Another compelling reason to control anger concerns the negative consequences that result from expressing anger inappropriately. In the extreme, angering may lead to violence or physical aggression, which can result in numerous negative consequences such as being arrested or jailed, being physically injured, being retaliated against, losing loved ones, being terminated from a substance abuse treatment or social service program, or feeling guilt, shame, or regret.

Even when angering does not lead to violence, the inappropriate expression of anger, such as verbal abuse or intimidating or threatening behavior, often results in negative consequences. For example, it is likely that others will develop fear, resentment, and lack of trust toward those who subject them to angry outbursts, which may cause alienation from individuals such as family members, friends, and coworkers.

However, the expression of anger initially has many apparent payoffs. One payoff is being able to manipulate and control others through aggressive and intimidating behavior; others may choose to comply with the angry person's demands because they fear verbal threats or violence. Another payoff is the release of tension that occurs when one loses his or her temper and acts aggressively. The individual may feel better after an angry outburst, but everyone else may feel worse.

In the long term, however, these initial payoffs lead to negative consequences from the elements of the real world. For this reason, they are called *apparent* payoffs because the long-term negative consequences far outweigh the short-term gains. For example, consider a father who persuades his children to comply with his demands by using an angry tone of voice and threatening gestures. These behaviors imply to the children that they will receive physical harm if they are not obedient. The immediate payoff for the father is that the children obey his commands. The long-term consequence, however, may be that the children learn to fear or dislike him and become emotionally detached from him. As they grow older, they may avoid contact with him or refuse to see him altogether or they may just defy his orders and dare him to try to make them obey him. This often leads to physical confrontation and fighting. The real world of the community takes a dim view of this action and often separates the child from the parent. (See the *Recognizing Child Abuse* section of this book.) Actions of the community that can teach avoidance of such behavior are suggested in Chapter Three, "Community's Role in Happiness."

Where Does Anger Come From?

The things we would like, wish, hope, and prefer to have turn into things we believe we must, should, ought to, are entitled to, and demand to have. Would our lives be easier, better, and more pleasant if we got everything we thought we should? YES! But is that the real world in which we live? NO! The important thing to remember is that it is not written anywhere (except in our minds) that others must, or must not, do anything.

Entitlement

The belief that we are entitled to something means that it is *due* or *owed* to us. Examples: "I'm entitled to be treated fairly at all times." "I'm entitled to have a good paying job." "I'm entitled to be taken care of by others." "I'm entitled to have what I want, when I want it." These are true only if "I were God and ruled the world then I'd make it that way."

Control

When others do not do what we think they should, we often choose angering. We may have successfully convinced others to do as we wanted in the past, when we were children and our parents gave in to our angering actions. But there are at least three problems with believing that our angering is capable of controlling others. First, it overlooks the fact that others have freedom of choice and that their compliance with the demand represents merely their decision to comply and not that we forced them to comply. Second, simply because someone chooses to give in to the angry demand today does not mean that they will do so tomorrow. And, third, when others perceive that we are trying to control them, they often choose to behave the exact opposite of what we are demanding and commanding of them.

Control is a hideous form of aggression. Many people want the external power that comes from control of others to satisfy their *inner power* needs. I think that Choice Theory's power need is really an inner power need—the one that comes from having self-control, self-esteem, self-actualization, and self-worth. I do not think that we can substitute external power for inner power and successfully satisfy our basic power need. External power is like an addiction; the more we get, the more we want. Ultimately, we seek situations where we can control others because we feel we must have that sense of control to survive. Just look at many of the rich and powerful people in the world who flaunt their power to control others. External power does not bring happiness, but inner power can. External power and control are the basis for domestic violence and angering in the family. Internal power as shown by competence, accomplishment, achievement, recognition, impact, etc. is the basis for calmness and peace in the family. When some people believe that they are not handling a situation the way they want (competently), they anger.

Fantasy

Angering is a product of living in the world of *should* where things are perfectly right for us. They are perfect because they are exactly the way we think they should, must, and ought to be. We always get what we want, when we want it, without delay or interference from others. Hard work is always rewarded. People never lie or gossip. Parents love and support their children, and children love and obey their parents.

The real world is different from the ideal world. Life is not always fair. We treat people well but they do not always treat us well in return. We work hard and have to wait for any kind of reward. Bad things sometimes do happen to good people.

Shame

Shame is the result of a strong sense of guilt, embarrassment or disgrace, the feeling that we get when we think that we did something wrong. Shame is what we feel when our inappropriate behavior is uncovered for all to see. We experience the emotion when we are laid bare psychologically as the world passes judgment on the choices we have made. Rather than continue to experience shame, some individuals choose to transform the emotion into anger. This angering, often directed towards those who have discovered them, allows them to feel powerful and potent again when their shame had made them feel powerless.

Stress

Mental health, too, is something to consider when assessing sources of anger, and dealing with stress in particular is something worth practicing. Fortunately, or unfortunately, most of us have ample opportunity to do so. Modern life is a veritable testing and proving ground for stress management, and both the experts and the general public are learning more about it every year.

Stress is an unavoidable part of life. We face it in our homes, at work, and even at play. We have to cope with it at every stage of our lives, from childhood and adolescence to adulthood and old age. If managed well, stress can be a great boon that spurs us on to achieve our goals and to live more fully. If poorly managed, though, it can cause a host of problems, from chronic anxiety to ulcers and mental breakdowns.

Stress itself is not necessarily unhealthy; it is our inappropriate total behaviors in dealing with it that causes the real-world reactions we call problems. A stressful situation for one person may be a stimulating experience for another, especially when in the close proximity of a family. One member of the family may enjoy loud rock music while another can hardly stand it. One member of the family may get the jitters thinking about giving a speech while another sees speechmaking as an exciting opportunity. Even positive experiences cause stress. The difference between the perceived world and the quality world brings about the stress and frustration in our lives.

In large part, the chosen total behavior to the stressor comes from our behavioral system. A new job may be unusually stressful at first because we want to be competent; we choose to add new, unaccustomed demands on ourselves. But with time we may get an understanding of what to do and find it very stimulating and satisfying. This comes from changes in the perceived world and quality world of the job. It is the same thing with survival. A person who has been through an emergency situation, or even rehearsed for it, will react more positively to survival stress than a person who has not.

Stress management is a popular term today. To alleviate the things that go wrong with our bodies and minds, we try everything from aspirin and tranquilizers to biofeedback machines and psychiatrists. All of these things have their place and I do not mean to make light of the good they can do if wisely used on a temporary basis. But the long-term answers to our frustrations and stressors are found in the changes we make in ourselves and in the way we relate to others in our lives.

Stress management begins with sensitivity to our own minds and bodies. It begins by standing aside and looking at our situation and asking ourselves, "Is my total behavior getting me what I want in this situation? If not, ask, "What do I need to change so that it does?" In some cases, it may mean simply getting used to an unfamiliar situation. In others, it may mean deleting some activities so that we can effectively deal with things that are more important.

One of the most interesting discoveries researchers have made regarding stress is that those who have a feeling of control in their lives experience far fewer stressful effects. People who have chosen to work in noisy offices and who know they have the freedom to leave at any time do not get nearly as upset as those who feel they must simply endure the discomfort. Similarly, people tend to accept stressful situations much more gracefully if they feel there is a purpose to them. The pain and shock of a necessary and carefully planned surgery is far less stressful than an equal amount of pain and shock caused by a sudden accident.

One of the greatest tools in stress management is advance planning. This can be done quite deliberately, simply by monitoring the number and type of changes in our lives. In a study first published in the *Journal of Psychosomatic Research* in 1967, Drs. T.H. Holmes and R.H. Rahe discovered that people who experienced many life changes over a short period of time were much more likely to get seriously ill or injured than those who experienced very few changes. Surprisingly, it made little difference whether those changes were positive or negative. A marriage was as stressful as a broken leg. A business promotion was as emotionally difficult as dealing with bothersome in-laws.

As part of their study, these doctors developed a Social Readjustment Rating Scale so that people could assess changes in their lives and plan ahead to minimize illness. Starting with a 10 percent chance of serious illness, whether you have any points or not (just through virtue of being alive), the authors arrive at a prediction of the chance of having a serious illness. If the total is less than 150, we have about a 33 percent chance of winding up in the hospital during the next two years. If the total is between 150 and three hundred, our chances of serious illness or injury increase to 50 percent. If the total is more than three hundred, our chances of a serious health problem over the next two years rise to as much as 90 percent. The highest event, the death of a spouse, is worth one hundred points. The lowest event, minor violation of the law, is worth eleven points. There are 43 different events rated in the study.

Aside from making changes in our lives, there are many other things we can do to minimize the effects of stress. Exercise is a wonderful antidote. Taking a walk for fifteen minutes can relieve tremendous amounts of pent-up energy. So can working in the yard, doing relaxation exercises, or any of the other methods discussed in this and other books.

This information is simple, concise, and easy to give and to learn, but the real personal challenge comes in implementing the changes in our lifestyle on a regular basis to gain the benefit from them and to reduce our reactivity to the stresses in our lives. This is something that Lute, in Appendix A, was unable to achieve. It is said that the hardest eighteen inches to traverse is from the knowledge in our heads to the belief system in our hearts (quality world). This is especially true in the heat of the battle, so to speak. Dealing with the stress levels is much like dealing with the anger levels discussed in Chapter Five, "Anger Management." The objective is to realize that the stress level is building toward the point of no return and to deal with the stressors before we reach the overload condition. When the point of no return is reached, severe reactions to stressors are inevitable.

Myths about Anger

Myths about angering provide excuses and misconceptions that allow for the continued use of the action of anger in the family.

Anger Is Inherited.

One misconception or myth about anger is that the way we express anger is inherited and cannot be changed. Sometimes, we may hear someone say, "I inherited my anger from my father; that's just the way I am." This statement implies that the expression of anger is a fixed and unalterable set of behaviors. Evidence from research studies, however, indicates that we are not born with set, specific ways of expressing anger. These studies show, rather, that because the expression of anger is a learned behavior, more appropriate ways of expressing anger also can be learned.

It is well established that much of our behavior is learned by observing others, particularly influential people. These people include parents, family members, and friends. If children observe parents expressing anger through aggressive acts such as verbal abuse and violence, it is very likely that they will learn to express anger in similar ways. Fortunately, this behavior can be changed by learning new and appropriate ways of anger expression. It is not necessary to continue to express anger by aggressive and violent means.

Anger Automatically Leads to Aggression.

A related myth involves the misconception that the only effective way to express anger is through aggression. It is commonly thought that anger is something that builds and escalates to the point of an aggressive outburst. As has been said, however, anger does not necessarily lead to aggression. In fact, effective anger management involves controlling the escalation of anger by learning assertiveness skills, changing negative and hostile self-talk, challenging irrational beliefs, and employing a variety of behavioral strategies. These skills, techniques, and strategies are discussed in group sessions with both domestic violence perpetrators and in parenting groups with parents. Assertive behavior was defined by Alberti and Emmonds (1974) as that which "enables a person to act in his own best interest, to stand up for himself without undue anxiety, to express his honest feelings comfortably, or to exercise his own rights without denying the right to others.... Get what you want without hurting others." When children learn this from their parents, they can maintain calmness and peace for the rest of their lives.

People Must Be Aggressive to Get What They Want.

Many people confuse assertiveness with aggression. The goal of aggression is to dominate, intimidate, harm, or injure another person—to win at any cost. Conversely, the goal of assertiveness is to express feelings of anger in a way that is respectful of other people. For example, if someone were upset because a friend was repeatedly late for dates or meetings, they could respond with name-calling and shouted obscenities. This approach is an attack on the other person rather than an attempt to address the behavior that one finds frustrating or anger provoking.

An assertive way of handling this situation might be to say, "When you are late for a meeting with me, I get pretty frustrated. I wish that you would be on time more often." This statement expresses your feelings of frustration and dissatisfaction and communicates how you would like the situation changed. This expression does not blame or threaten the other person and minimizes the chance of causing emotional harm. We discuss assertiveness skills in more detail in group sessions. All assertiveness includes use of the caring habits.

Venting Anger Is Always Desirable.

For many years, the popular belief among mental health professionals and laymen was that the aggressive expression of anger, such as screaming or beating on pillows, was healthy and therapeutic. Research studies have found, however, that people who vent their anger aggressively simply get better at being angry (Berkowitz, 1970; Murray, 1985; Straus, Gelles, & Steinmetz, 1980). In other words, venting anger in an aggressive manner reinforces aggressive behavior. Defusing the anger with the use of adjusted thinking and positive physical exercise is a far superior method of dealing with the stress and aggravation that comes from not being able to control the situation.

Lies We Tell Ourselves to Justify Our Anger

People tell themselves lies to justify their anger so that they can continue to act out against others. The following are six lies that are often used.

If I do not get angry and behave aggressively, people will think I'm a wimp and walk all over me.

Many people rely on angering as a way of countering the perceptions that others think they are weak. Gang members often tell each other this common lie. The problem with this approach is that, if someone is determined to view you as weak, all the anger and aggression we can generate will not necessarily change his or her view of us. As a matter of fact, others will actually point to our anger as proof that we are weak and out of control. As you will learn, being able to choose your total behavior, including reactions other than anger, is a sign of strength, not weakness.

I just get angry. I have no control over my emotions.

The notion of being able to choose our emotional response in a particular situation sounds strange at first. Throughout our lives we have been taught that emotions are things that happen to us and, as such, are beyond our control. Nothing, however, could be farther from the truth. Emotions, as my clients learn, are products of how one thinks and acts in specific situations. Clients learn that, to the extent that they control their thoughts and actions, so, too, can they exercise control over their emotions as part of their total behavior.

Only by expressing my anger am I going to feel better. I should never keep my anger bottled up.

While people who chronically choose to anger are more likely to experience certain physical problems than their counterparts who do not choose to anger, that does not mean that the solution to the anger problem involves spewing anger out every time they experience it. The reality is that there are countless examples of people they are better off not expressing anger towards—spouses, children, police officers, employers, judges, and gangsters brandishing guns. Rather than struggling not to act out your angering, or surrendering to it, people need to learn to manage their anger to avoid both the physical problems associated with its repression as well as the personal and interpersonal problems associated with its expression.

There is no such thing as healthy anger.

As with other emotional choices (i.e., to depress or to elevate our levels of anxiety), angering can be viewed as conveying information concerning the current state of a person's perceived world as compared with their quality world. Anger can alert us to problems in that comparison that needs to be solved. Used in this way, angering can be helpful and, in that respect, healthy. People who use Choice Theory use their angering this way. Others may believe that healthy irritation helps us overcome life's problems, while intense feelings of anger will always cause more problems. This belief leads to a partial solution, but Choice Theory can bring more happiness to the person who lives by its concepts. Their family finds calmness and peace.

Hitting something, like a pillow, will help me deal better with my anger.

There is no evidence to support the value of *letting off steam* as the best way to deal with anger. In fact, evidence suggests that this is the wrong way to learn angering control. If we hit a pillow, we may feel better immediately after discharging our anger. Unfortunately, rather than dealing with the anger in constructive ways, we are simply rehearsing future aggressive behaviors. In cases like this, we recall the momentary relief we experience after behaving aggressively. That split-second of relief reinforces the aggressive behavior, and consequently, we tend to behave this way in the future. This sense of immediate relief is also easily transferable from hitting inanimate objects to hitting people.

I cannot help it if other people or situations make me angry.

This is the greatest lie of all. How many times have you said to yourself, "(Fill in the blank) makes me so angry!" or "I would not have gotten angry if (fill in the blank) had done what he said he would do!" Do you see any problems with believing that other people make you angry? As long as you believe that other people make you angry, they are in control of you and your emotions! As long as you believe that other people make you angry, you are powerless over your anger! To be in control of your total behavior, to regain your personal power, it is essential that you abandon the notion that others *make* you angry and replace it with the proposition that only you are powerful enough to choose your own feelings and how to deal with them.

To What End Does Angering Lead?

The above myths and lies lead to the choice to continue angering, and the action of expressing anger can have many negative consequences for the angry person.

Angering can kill you.

Research clearly demonstrates that persons unable to manage their angering are at greater risk for heart disease, high blood pressure, headaches, strokes, and stomach-related problems. Studies suggest that those people reporting higher levels of angering at age twenty-five are four to seven times more likely to be dead by age fifty than those reporting lower levels of angering.

Angering destroys your most important relationships.

No one enjoys being around a person when they are angering. In fact, most people are afraid of angering people. When people use the deadly habits while angering, it pushes others away and further isolates the angry person from the world. Angering destroys the calm and peace that a family should have.

Society punishes people who anger and act aggressively.

If a person is unable to manage his or her anger and the aggressive actions growing out of that anger, society, through its legal mechanisms, will attempt to control the actions for him or her—most likely in ways the angering person will not like. No matter how self-righteous or justified the person might believe the anger to be, society will punish him or her, especially if the anger turns into aggression. Family members will distance themselves from the angering person.

Life will find ways to punish people for their angry actions.

This is a somewhat philosophical observation, but one that an angry person understands almost immediately. Opportunities that may have materialized, had a person been less aggressive, pass them by. Doors that may have opened, because of their skills or knowledge, remain closed because others fear being exposed to excessive aggression. The love and belonging of the family is illusive and there is little peace in the family.

Angering leads to decreased problem solving. Angering leads to verbal and physical aggression.

Three Forms of Angering

There are three forms of angering: passive, passive-aggressive, and aggressive. These three forms are used in varying ways to express the frustration and displeasure over a situation.

Passive

Passive behaviors are the opposite of aggressive behaviors. Instead of harming others either physical or verbally, we allow others to run us over without protesting. Instead of stating our thoughts, feelings, and wishes we remain silent and allow others to push us around.

Passive-aggressive

Passive-aggressive behaviors involve an indirect expression of anger. Rather than coming out and saying that we are angry, we let people know through our tone of voice and other behaviors such as sulking, pouting, or giving someone the cold shoulder or silent treatment. And example of passive-aggressive behavior would be for a husband to drop the dishes after the wife insisted that he help her by drying them. After one or two dropped dishes, the wife will take the towel away from him and tell him to sit down while she does the job.

Aggressive

Aggressive behaviors include hitting things, hitting other people, verbally beating other people up, and threatening people. They are designed to intimidate and control others by force, regardless of the costs. When aggression is chosen, people are likely to speak in a loud voice and get up in the other person's face while making their demands.

Family Aggression Awareness

"Domestic violence is not simply a private family matter—it is a matter affecting the entire community. Too many of America's homes have become places where *women, children, and seniors suffer physical abuse and emotional trauma.* Domestic violence is a leading cause of injury to women in our country, and it occurs among all racial, ethnic, religious, and economic groups. It is a particularly devastating form of abuse because it wears a familiar face: the face of a spouse, parent, partner or child. This violence too often extends beyond the home and into the workplace."—President Clinton's proclamation of National Domestic Violence Awareness Month, October 1, 1997. (Italics added by author to indicate an implied definition of *domestic violence* or *family aggression* that involves the entire family.)

The California Penal Code defines abuse as "intentionally or recklessly causing or attempting to cause bodily injury, or placing another person in reasonable apprehension of imminent, serious bodily injury to himself, herself, or another." Domestic violence is the term applied if a person is abused by a spouse or former spouse, someone he or she lives with or used to live with, someone he or she is dating or engaged to, or someone with whom he or she has had a child. Therefore, family aggression and domestic violence refer to the same actions in the home environment.

The Domestic Violence Intervention Project (DVIP) defines domestic violence or family aggression as "the systematic use of violence and abuse to gain power over and to control a partner or ex-partner. Domestic violence occurs across all cultures, ages, ethnic groups and social classes. As well as covering physical violence—including all forms of aggressive or unwanted physical contact and sexual violence—domestic violence includes non-physical abuse such as verbal, social, racist, psychological, or emotional abuse, threats, neglect, harassment, and the use of economic, structural, institutional, or even spiritual abuse."

Some of the characteristics of family aggression or domestic violence follow:

- Your partner hits, kicks, slaps, or shoves you, or has an explosive temper; throws things at you or breaks things in anger; criticizes, threatens or blames you frequently; or tries to control your behavior or forces you to have sex.

- You change your behavior because you are afraid that violence might result if you do not.

- You often have the feeling of *walking on eggshells*.

- You feel that no matter what you do, you can not do anything right. Your partner tells you that you are worthless, unattractive, that no one else would want you.

- Your spouse abuses drugs or alcohol and becomes out of control, gets extremely angry, and then tries to make up afterwards. You constantly worry about the next time he or she gets high.

- Your partner tries to keep you from getting medical help.

- The abuser prevents you from sleeping at night or you are worried about being attacked in your sleep.
- Your partner is extremely jealous. Your intimate partner unjustly accuses you of flirting with others or having affairs. It is hard for you to maintain relationships with others because your intimate partner does not approve of them.
- Your partner sometimes spends large sums of money and refuses to tell you why or on what the money was spent. You do not know what the family's assets are and where important records are kept.
- Your partner frequently threatens you with never seeing your children again if you leave, because his or her sex always wins the custody of children.

Other facts about aggressive angering:

- Aggressive angering is unacceptable behavior.
- The right to live free from intimidation, abuse, and violence is a basic human right.
- Aggressive angering is very common.
- Aggressive angering is very dangerous—the aggressor is 100 percent responsible for his or her abusive behavior.
- Aggressive angering is not the fault or responsibility of the victim— no victim ever deserves to be abused no matter what he or she says or does.
- Violence towards a partner or child is intentional and instrumental behavior—it is about an aggressor controlling the partner's or child's behavior and establishing the power to set the rules within the relationship.
- Violence towards a partner or child is learned behavior.

- Aggressive angering between partners and children in a relationship may be triggered by numerous factors, including stressful or frustrating life situations such as loss of a job; financial problems or pregnancy; role changes that may impact the batterer's sense of control; use of alcohol and/or drug abuse, which may increase abusive behavior; attitudes and beliefs on the part of the batterer that rationalize abuse; sadistic personality of the batterer; and mental or physical disorders.

- Aggressive angering is rooted in power inequalities within historical and institutional power structures in society.

- Aggressors can change—their behavior is within their control and they can choose to stop—however, making changes is far from easy and many aggressors do not have sufficient motivation.

- Victims cannot stop the aggressor's violence—but there may be things they can do to increase their own and their children's safety.

Between three and ten million children in the United States each year observe abuse of one parent by the other. Violence in the family is a major contributor to the abuse of children. Every one of the children in a violent family is aware of the violence and is affected in some manner. Understanding the aspects of violence in the family can reduce or possibly eliminate this abuse. Additionally, peace and stability can be enjoyed by all members of the family, fostering a more calm and safe home environment. If the aspects of violence in the family can be understood and reduced or eliminated, peace, calm, and stability can be provided for the children.

Aggressive behavior is the hallmark of *external control psychology*. It represents an attempt to solve problems by imposing one's will on others and pressuring them to do what you want. Aggression is satisfying to the offender because it produces a measure of power. However, it is only marginally satisfying because aggression separates the parties from one another and the love and belonging needs of all family members suffer. Marginally satisfying aggressive behavior usually progresses to levels that are more serious. What begins as a hostile or threatening attitude develops over time into overtly abusive behavior.

In homes where domestic violence or family aggression occurs between partners, children are at high risk of suffering physical abuse themselves. The children learn that aggression is the solution to many of their problems and it becomes a need-satisfying behavior for them. The American Humane Society (1994) found that women who have been beaten by their spouses are twice as likely as other women to abuse their children. Regardless of whether children are physically abused, the emotional effects of witnessing family aggression are very similar to the psychological trauma associated with being a victim of child abuse. Children in homes where family aggression occurs are physically abused or seriously neglected at a rate 1,500 percent higher than the average in the general population (Center For The Prevention of Domestic Violence, 1997). Donna Wills, chief district attorney of the Los Angeles County Family Violence Unit, reports that 90 percent of all death row offenders allege family aggression or child abuse in their background (Wills, 1995). The California State Child Abuse Laws (Welfare & Institutions Code 300) allow for the removal of children from a domestically violent home based on the assumption that the children will experience emotional abuse and be at high risk of physical abuse.

A comparison of delinquent and non-delinquent youth revealed that a history of family violence or abuse is the most significant difference between the two groups.

Aggression in the family or domestic violence is a major problem in our society today. In a national survey of over six thousand American families, 50 percent of the men who frequently assaulted their wives also frequently abused their children. More children are served in battered women's shelters than are adults. Children are present in more than half of the homes where police are called for domestic violence.

Counseling aggressive people with external control methods is using force to deal with force and it can lead to more anger within the aggressor. The courts order the clients to come to counseling to learn how to live without angering and violence and how to parent their children in a non-aggressive manner. As a result of these orders, the clients usually choose to be angry at the courts and resent having to be in the group. This further perpetuates their resentment of external control and the system. They arrive at counseling sessions blaming the partner, law enforcement, the district attorney, the public defender, the court, and anyone else they can blame—everyone except themselves.

There are three categories of aggressors: *family only, generally violent,* and *emotionally volatile.* The *family only* aggressors are least likely to be violent outside the home. The *generally violent* aggressors are most likely to be violent outside the home. The *emotionally volatile* aggressors are angry, depressed, and jealous. They exhibit some physical violence and much psychological abuse.

Common characteristics of all abusers:

- Use projection (blaming the mate for the marital strife or the child for not obeying).
- Disallow mate's or child's autonomy (mate or child can only be a possession or an extension of their ego).
- Consider mate or child to be a symbol (mate or child is not a person but a symbol of someone or something else).
- Demands that mate adheres to expectations of marriage (demands that both adhere to the aggressor's original expectation of what a marriage is like).
- Possesses attractive characteristics (no one is totally evil or vicious).
- Lacks intimacy (unable to attain the mutuality of a truly intimate relationship).

Power and Control Wheel

The power and control wheel from *Power and Control,* by E. Pence and M. Paymar (1986), and the Domestic Abuse Intervention Project in Duluth, Minn., shows how abusive partners use different forms of sexual, social, and psychological abuse to maintain power and control. Once this pattern has begun, it will cycle around again until the threat of physical abuse begins to overshadow all aspects of a battered person's life. The original wheel contains eight elements. I have added minimizing, denying, and blaming as elements to the wheel. Though developed to describe the attributes of power and control that men use over women, it also applies to the power and control that parents try to maintain over their children. It is easy to expand each of the descriptions to actions used with children. The descriptions of each element have been adapted from the original wheel to include these expansions.

Isolation

Isolation by controlling what she does, whom she sees and talks to, what she reads, where she goes, limits the victim's outside involvement. The batterer uses jealousy to justify his actions and keep his partner from having male friends. Isolation keeps her from others who could support her and elevate her self-worth. When both partners are at a party, isolation is demonstrated when the batterer refuses to let the woman talk with other guests or accuses her of flirting with the other men at the party.

With children, isolation includes not letting them play and socialize with other children and requiring them to come home directly after school.

Emotional Abuse

Emotional abuse includes putting the woman down or making her feel bad about herself by calling her names, making her think she is crazy, and playing mind games with her by humiliating her and making her feel guilty. An example of this would be to show her off to your friends as beautiful and then, in private, telling her that she dresses in the same manner as a whore.

For children, this might include praising them to people outside of the family while, at home, blaming them for all of the family's problems, stress, and angering.

Intimidation

After watching looks, anger, gestures, loud voice, smashing things or destroying property it is understandable for one to choose to be intimidated and fearful. Abusing pets can intimidate her. Displaying weapons in a threatening manner so that she may think that he might use them against her intimidates her.

Each of our parents had *that look* that told us we were in trouble. An example of intimidation is counting with the threat of physical punishment if the child does not do what you want by the time you reach the magic number.

Economic Abuse

Economic abuse includes trying to keep her from getting or keeping a job or making her ask for money, giving her an allowance, or taking the money she earns for your own use. There are many ways of not letting her know about or have access to family income and these are all economic abuse.

Economic abuse takes place when parents refuse to let the child have some discretion and choice over how money is spent on him or her.

Using Male Privilege

Treating the woman like a servant is using male privilege to control her. Making all the *big* decisions is another way of expressing male privilege. Other expressions of male privilege include acting like, or stating that you are the *master of the castle* or being the one to define man's and woman's roles. Male privilege includes having different rules in the home for the man than for the woman, such as having a *night out with the boys* but not allowing her to have an *evening with her girlfriends*.

Boys have different rules than girls in the home. "Boys will be boys, but girls have to be protected."

Sexual Abuse

Sexual abuse includes making her do sexual things against her will. This can include making her dress like a sex object in revealing clothing that she does not want to wear. Physically attacking the sexual parts of her body or treating her like a sex object are also examples of sexual abuse.

The same things apply to sexual abuse of children.

Coercion and Threats

Coercion is the making and/or carrying out threats to hurt her emotionally. Examples include threatening to take the children, commit suicide, or report her to welfare; making her drop charges of domestic violence; or making her do illegal things that put her in jeopardy of going to jail.

Telling the children they will be put in foster homes if they tell anyone about what happens in the home is abuse.

Using Children

When the abuser uses the children to make the spouse feel guilty about the family situation or the way she parents them, the children are being used to control her. *Triangling* is the use of the children to give messages instead of talking directly to your partner about problems. Abusing visitation orders by not letting her see the children when you are separated is a way to harass her. Threatening to take the children away when you are talking about separating is another way to pressure her to do as you want and control her. Another way to use children is to turn them against their mother by telling them lies about her.

The situation in reverse can be used against children, when the abuser tells them they cannot see their mother if they do not obey.

Minimizing, Denying, and Blaming

Making light of the abuse and not taking her concerns about it seriously is one way of controlling the family situation. Saying the abuse did not happen or denying that there was any abuse weakens her support system. Shifting responsibility for abusive behavior to her or the children instead of taking responsibility is a way of blaming the battered spouse or the children for angering in the family. Saying she or the children caused the fight and that it is their fault that the batterer is angering is directly blaming the abuser's behavior on them.

These nine elements lead to all forms of *physical abuse*, such as pushing, shoving, hitting, slapping, choking, pulling hair, twisting arms, tripping, biting, beating, throwing her down, using a weapon, punching, kicking, and grabbing, which can be used against both spouses and children.

Additional characteristics of aggressors include:

- Jealousy,
- Controlling behavior,
- A short engagement or relationship before moving in with a mate or partner,
- Unrealistic expectations of the relationship,
- Blaming others for their own problems and feelings,
- Being supersensitive,
- Verbally abusive,
- Making threats of physical violence toward the mate, family, and others.

Equality Wheel

The equality wheel, developed by the Domestic Abuse Intervention Project, shows how nonviolent partners use different forms of caring habits to live a nonviolent lifestyle. Once this pattern has begun, it can bring peace and love back to all aspects of a victim's life. The wheel contains eight elements. These elements apply to the relationship with children as well as that with the partner. The descriptions of each element have been adapted from the original wheel to include the concepts of Choice Theory.

Negotiation and Fairness

Negotiation and fairness include seeking mutually satisfying resolutions to conflict, accepting changes, and being willing to compromise.

Non-threatening Behavior

Examples of non-threatening behavior are listening, supporting, caring, talking and acting so that partners feel safe and comfortable expressing themselves and doing things.

Respect

Show respect for your partner by listening non-judgmentally, being emotionally affirming and understanding, and valuing your partner's opinions.

Economic Partnership

Economic partnership includes making money decisions together and making sure both partners benefit from financial arrangements.

Trust and Support

Supporting your partner's goals in life shows your trust. Respecting your partner's right to his or her own feelings, friends, activities, and opinions is supportive of your partner's individuality.

Shared Responsibility

Examples of sharing responsibility include mutually agreeing on a fair distribution of work and making family decisions together.

Responsible Parenting

Parental responsibilities need to be shared and mutual. Parents should be positive, nonviolent role models for the children.

Honesty and Accountability

Choice Theory centers on accepting responsibility for yourself and your total behavior. Acknowledging past use of violence, admitting being wrong, and communicating openly and truthfully are ways of being honest and accountable.

Children of battering families are physically abused and neglected at a rate up to fifteen times higher than the national average. Their brains form differently from the brains of children who grow up in families that are not anger driven. They learn that the world is not a safe place to live in, and not to trust anyone. This is the most difficult belief to change when the child becomes an adult and tries to change into a caring person. In addition to any physical or sexual abuse children may be subjected to, they are aware of the violence directed at their parent(s). The tension in the home results in poor schooling and other areas of neglect. Children who witnessed abuse of their caretaker were twenty-four times more likely to commit sexual assault crimes; 50 percent more likely to abuse drugs and/or alcohol; 74 percent more likely to commit crimes against another person; and six times more likely to commit suicide.

Self-discipline or self-control is a term that we use daily and think that we understand. The roots of the word discipline are found in the word disciple. To be a disciple means to be "one who embraces and assists in spreading the teaching of another." Thus, to be a disciple means not only to be a kind of follower, but also to be a teacher. I consider myself to be a disciple of Choice Theory. Self-control is a form of self-teaching, self-instruction or self-regulation. For most of us, the first disciples or teachers in our lives are our parents.

Parents need to first instruct themselves in self-control before attempting to instruct their children. How many parents do you know who demonstrate self-control? Do *you* operate from a position of self-control? How many parents believe that they are capable of disciplining their children when they are themselves undisciplined?

When we are having difficulty with our children, the first place we need to look for answers is in the mirror. Rather than focusing energy on trying to change or control the children, look to see how you can change yourself. If we cannot manage ourselves, how can we teach our children to manage themselves? When we are managing our anger, we are practicing self-control. Children see this self-control, respect it, and seek to emulate us. Once we have disciplined ourselves, only then are we ready to discipline our children.

A relationship exists between anger and poor parenting skills (i.e., external control or relying primarily on punishment as the means of getting children to alter their behavior). A similar relationship exists between Choice Theory and improved parenting skills (i.e., relying primarily on the relationship with your children as the means of influencing them to make the choice to alter their behavior). Influencing children is not the same as punishing them. Punishment is a behavior growing out of anger. It is designed solely to reduce the occurrence of certain behaviors with which you, as a parent, do not agree. When we are angry and thinking only of punishing our child, we deprive them of the opportunity to learn as much as they can from their experiences. Helping them learn from their experiences and influencing them from our behavior are goals of Choice Theory parenting.

Children who learn to accept violence as a means of conflict resolution often fail to develop their own inner controls. They learn to maintain control of others by using threats of violence. They learn that loved ones have the right to hurt one another. They often feel guilty for the violence between their parents or for the violence toward themselves. They feel angry toward one or both parents. They experience anxiety and fear. They often protect the abuser in the face of outside intervention. They have sleep disturbances such as bed-wetting, nightmares, and insomnia. They have difficulties in school such as staying awake, concentrating on work, and playing with peers. These children are often diagnosed with ADHD or ADD and then medicated. They have poor appetites. They often confuse love with violence. They learn unhealthy sex-role stereotypes from their parents. And they grow up to be abusers of their own mates and children.

Parenting is not an easy job. It takes patience, creativity, and an endless amount of love and understanding. Some parenting skills come naturally; however, many need to be learned. The same can be said of being a child. Their curiosity is natural; however, self-discipline must be learned. As parents, we are responsible for teaching self-discipline to our children. It takes time and practice—but it does get easier—as children learn their own self-discipline. It does not have to hurt our children or us. Chapter Six, "Helping Children Become Adults—Parenting," addresses violence and discipline in the family. Much of the violence is aggression in the name of influence or discipline. This book does not go into parenting techniques in additional detail because it is intended to provide the underlying philosophy that will make those techniques useful and successful. See some of the many available parenting books and articles for a more complete discussion on parenting techniques.

CHAPTER 3

Community's Role in Happiness

Researchers have found a clear inverse relationship between parental attitudes toward violence and their children's history of fighting. The more accepting the parent is toward violence, the more prone the child is to engage in violent scuffles. Similar results are found for the use of corporal punishment, such as spanking, in the home.

The results are interesting but predictable, says Daniel W. Webster (HealthDay *Monday*, Feb. 6, 2006), associate professor at the Center for the Prevention of Youth Violence, part of the Johns Hopkins Bloomberg School of Public Health in Baltimore. "It is very consistent with other research about the cycle of violence," he said. "In homes where there is physical violence between parents, or parent to child, that increases the likelihood that they will have problems with increased violence." Webster stressed, however, that most children who do experience violence do not go on to violence—but it certainly increases the risk.

Steve Lopez (*Los Angeles Times*, Dec. 12, 2005) reporter for the Los Angeles Times states, "People are locked up for being mentally ill, essentially, because there is nowhere else to put them. The jail is a dumping bin, teeming with inmates. The jailers are ill-equipped and too understaffed to help, and sometimes can't even protect." In the same article, Los Angeles County Sheriff Baca points out that in a better system, the mentally ill would not have gone to jail. Lopez continues, "All mental health services are in absurdly short supply. The state (California) mental hospitals are ridiculously understaffed and often chaotic and dangerous. Community clinics are few and far between.... The jailhouse is one of the few places where mental health care is available.… What I've learned about mental illness is that there are no cures, and there are no easy fixes, either, for a system that's been shamefully neglected for decades."

Carla Mia DiMassa (*Los Angeles Times*, Dec. 24, 2005) reporter for the Loa Angeles Times states, "A patchwork system of mental heath care and medical services for the indigent often fails some of society's most desperate, virtually ensuring deaths" to those whom it tries to serve. "Traditional clinics and hospitals frequently are not equipped to deal with mental illness. Mental hospitals do not necessarily have facilities to handle acute physical illness." Referring to the people who need more than just one isolated service, the Director of Los Angeles County Department of Mental Health, Marvin Southard, states, "The health system does not work very well for such people."

Dr. Glasser (1998A) states that in a caring or quality community, family violence would be minimized because the community would go beyond the efforts of any single program. Instead, it would teach Choice Theory and use what he calls a solving circle—a method of discussing and solving problems within a family or group of people. This would prevent a great deal of family—spousal and child—disagreements that later escalate to violence. Dr. Glasser suggests that if family violence had reached a level such that the police or children's services were involved; the family would be advised to enter a nonpunitive, educational intervention program that would teach effective methods of dealing with family violence without the use of imprisonment or fines. The key to dealing with all violence is early intervention before much harm is done or before jail becomes the only choice the judge has.

In a quality community, as soon as anyone found out that a child was being mistreated at home or was not getting along at school or in the community; it would be considered a community emergency. Most adolescents who are in serious trouble are known to the community before they do anything criminal. Early intervention would prevent suffering and costly intervention by the community. This concept is in opposition to what communities do now—punish or neglect—which does not work. Things only get worse.

A list of involvement areas was developed by Mike Jackson and David Oarvin of the Domestic Violence Institute of Michigan as a set of elements in a program dealing with male violence against females. The original list focused on men's aggression against women, but I have modified and expanded it to deal with all external control and aggression, independent of the age or gender of the aggressor or victim. I have also combined the response with the action model to form a more complete list of community involvement suggestions. These elements include the people that Dr. Glasser suggested should be included in groups that initiate a quality community.

1. We, the people
2. Educational system
3. Social service providers
4. Justice system
5. Health care system
6. Government
7. Employers
8. Clergy
9. Media.

One issue in our current system is lack of *communication* between each of the elements. *Confidentiality* of the information is important for the protection of personal data, but it is often the reason that information is not shared between the various departments. In a quality community, as soon as anyone found out that a child was having difficulty, the problem would be addressed by all of the systems involved with the family. With communication, the departments could work together to assist the person in making the changes necessary to bring about the happiness he or she deserves. In the example of Jeremy given in Appendix B, the Department of Mental Health did not share the information it gathered about Jeremy with the school or the social workers. Other interested parties do not have the information the department used in coming to its decision to aid Jeremy, even though the final decision was made available to the school, social workers, and community mental health workers without much regard to confidentiality. The Los Angeles County Department of Children and Family Services had a similar policy—the results are a matter of public record, but the investigation information is not shared with other agencies without a formal release of information. Both agencies could use this shared information to develop a coordinated effort to help Jeremy. The government and the justice system have, in their perception of mental health as a medical model instead of a public health problem, treated all of this information as though it were personal medical information. They have passed and enforced laws that protect patients from the unscrupulous sharing of this information (HIPAA Law) unless permission is given specifically by the parents or patient on a one-at-a-time need-to-know basis. Schools are told not to give the address and phone number of families to child abuse investigators without first obtaining written permission from the parents. This negates the element of unrehearsed testimony from the members of the family and jeopardizes the validity of the investigation and the safety of the children. It hinders the access of the parents and children to the investigators. Law enforcement personnel are not hampered by these regulations, but the police are not available to accompany investigators on every visit to a school.

A second suggestion that crosses all of the elements is *education. We, the people,* must realize that ignorance is the greatest supporter of violence and aggression against people by others and by the legal community against the law breakers. *Education* must be based on competence of understanding the information, not on passing any given test. *Education* must be used instead of punishment. The educational system is charged with educating the public, but it lacks an effective method for getting the knowledge to its students. The system of tests and failures does not work as effectively as would a model of learning to competence in a caring educational environment. It is not that the teachers in our communities do not care, but they are laboring under the false notion, directed by *government* laws, that placing more pressure on a student to pass a test will get better results. Do not we want our students to know the information instead of memorizing it for a test? The *social service providers* need to have educational capabilities to provide to their clients so that the clients can learn how to be more nurturing and caring to their charges. The charges also need to be exposed to less punishment and more correction with education.

The *justice system* must substitute education for punishment and separation from the community (confinement). All penal institutions should be schools, not just housing facilities. The inmates should be in classes to learn how to live in society without continuing to force their will on others. The Los Angeles County Sheriff's Office has a program named Bridges to Recovery. The program was developed by the Hacienda La Puente School District and is taught largely by three instructors. It teaches anger management in Lynwood's Century Regional Detention Facility to those inmates who are ready to change. The curriculum stresses self-discovery and self-control in typical life situations. Officials believe this program is helping inmates change their manner of dealing with the frustration of everyday life.

Jenifer Warren (*Los Angeles Times,* June 8, 2006, "High Cost of Prisons Not Paying Off, Report Finds") reports that "Americans spend $60 billion a year to imprison 2.2 million people—exceeding any other nation—but receive a dismal return on the investment, according to a report (Confronting Confinement, 2006), released by the Commission on Safety and Abuse in America's Prisons, urging greater public scrutiny of what goes on behind bars."

This is a report on violence and abuse in U.S. jails and prisons, the impact of those problems on public safety and public health, and how correctional facilities nationwide can become safer and more effective. Five members of the Commission have testified before the U.S. Senate Judiciary Subcommittee on Corrections and Rehabilitation about the report's key findings and recommendations.

The Commission recommends:

- A re-investment in programming for prisoners to prevent violence inside facilities and reduce recidivism after release;
- Changing federal law to extend Medicaid and Medicare reimbursement to correctional facilities and ending prisoner co-pays for medical care, reforms necessary to protect the public health;
- Reducing the use of high-security segregation, which can actually cause violence, and ending the release of prisoners directly from these units to the streets, which contributes to recidivism;
- Increasing investment at state and local levels to recruit, train, and retain skilled, capable workers at all levels;
- Expanding the capacity of the National Institute of Corrections to work with states and localities to create a positive institutional culture in corrections facilities;
- Creating an independent agency in every state to oversee prisons and jails and changing federal law to narrow the scope of the Prison Litigation Reform Act;
- Developing standardized reporting nationwide on violence and abuse behind bars so that corrections officials, lawmakers, and the public can have reliable measures of violence and monitor efforts to make facilities safer.

The *health care system* must stress public education about health matters. An example of the health care system doing this is in the smoking cessation effort. It has significantly reduced smoking in all portions of the community. In this effort, many of the elements worked together to achieve the desired goal of improved health and lifestyle. The *health care providers, government, employers, clergy,* and *media* have all been a part of the effort to educate the community about the dangers of smoking. This kind of coordinated effort needs to be mounted by the community against aggression—the number one problem in our communities and the root of failure in *we, the people,* living together in peace.

Last, but not least, *cooperation* between each of the elements is mandatory. As the example of Jeremy reveals, too many of the elements protect their territory and limit their participation in an overall solution. They become part of the problem instead of being part of the solution. Going the extra mile to cooperate with other systems brings about solutions instead of loopholes in which the clients become entrapped. Cooperation is not only a system element, but also the responsibility of the individual person within the system. The systems have to encourage cooperation instead of discourage it by establishing rules that hamper or forbid cooperation. The school personnel are taught by the justice system not to cooperate with the social services workers because the government has passed laws to punish those who share information without parental permission. The State of Tennessee is using cooperation in its program to identify drug offenders for public health reasons. Methamphetamine labs were becoming a public threat to the extent that residents could not even feel safe in their own homes. The chemicals in the drug are absorbed by concrete and plaster. Layers of topsoil must be removed in areas where chemicals were dumped. Children are being exposed to toxic hazards due to the manufacturing in the residential community. The state's website, Methamphetamine Offender Registry, allows Internet users to enter a name or a county and instantly obtain the convictions corresponding to the entry. This type of cooperation is the keystone of this coordinated action model.

We, the People

We, the people need to acknowledge that all users of external control benefit from aggression and violence and we need to be active in our opposition of external control. We need to use educational methods to advocate against all violence toward men, women, and children. We need to make peace, justice, and equality human virtues. We need vigorously to confront aggressors who indulge in deceptive behavior. We need to seek out and accept the leadership of all qualified people that support these needs and to reject those who do not support these needs as unqualified to lead us to the goals that we want. Most of all, we, the people, have to be willing to vote, not only at the polls, but also with our dollars, for the programs that will improve our communities, not just segregate the undesirables from the rest of us. Our financial support of community improvement programs is essential to create peace.

Educational System

Teachers and supporting school staff need to dialogue with students about violence in their homes, the dynamics of violence, and how it is founded on the oppression of one person at the expense of another. Quality schools as described by Dr. Glasser in *The Quality School* (1990) and *Every Student Can* Succeed (2000) would educate and demonstrate to the community the effectiveness of Choice Theory and the ultimate question. Researchers need to provide leadership in research and theoretical development that prioritizes gender and age justice, equal opportunity, and peace for all people. Teachers need to be supported and educated to recognize and respond to symptoms of violence in student's lives. The educational staff needs to intervene in harassment, abuse, violence, and intimidation of students and faculty in the educational system. Teachers need to teach violence prevention, peace-honoring conflict resolution, and communication skills as part of their everyday curriculum. Every student can succeed in the classroom if taught with success in mind instead of testing for failure. The teachers need to build competence that will eliminate both failure and discipline problems. Educators need to acknowledge gender bias in teaching materials and develop alternatives. Education about relationships at all levels, the civic duty of all citizens to oppose oppression, and the support of those who are oppressed, needs to be taught in each grade. Educators need to coordinate their efforts with other organizations regarding the investigation and activities to stem abuse and aggression, not only inside, but outside of the school setting as well.

Social Service Providers

Social workers need to become social change advocates for battered men, women, and children. They need to refer batterers to accountable intervention programs and stop blaming batterers' behavior on myths such as drugs and alcohol, family history, anger, provocation, loss of control, etc. Social workers need to design and deliver services that are sensitive to the safety needs of the victims and minimize how batterers use the services to continue abusing their families. Staff should be required to receive training on the etiology and dynamics of family aggression. Social service providers need to oppose the pathologizing of family aggression and shift the focus from trying to keep the family together at all costs to safety for battered men, women, and children. Social workers need to participate in the coordination of all agencies to bring about a community that is actively working to reduce aggression in all forms. The social service system needs to have educational programs available to provide to their clients. Finally, they need to help identify all forms of violence.

Justice System

The justice system, which includes the law enforcement system, the probation system, the court system, and the penal system, needs to adopt mandatory arrest policies for those who batter and to refer batterers exclusively to intervention programs that meet state or federal standards. Make those standards general and not program-specific and make standards that are suitable for adults and youth. Delayed or deferred sentence options to batterers should never be offered. Easily accessible protection orders need to be provided and then they need to be backed up with rapid response by law enforcement. Incarcerate the adult batterer for noncompliance with any aspect of his or her adjudication and re-evaluate the youth program for the youth who re-offend. The justice system needs to vigorously enforce batterers' compliance, and protect victims and their children's safety, with custody, visitation, and injunctive orders. Law enforcement needs to adopt a *pro-education policy* independent of the sex or age of the aggressor. Since punishment has been proven to be ineffective as a method of change, education should be mandatory while the convicted are in custody. Who can say that education is *cruel and unusual punishment*? All police and correctional officers should be offered the opportunity to learn the concepts of the Quality Community and the ultimate question as part of Choice Theory. Judges in a Quality Community would find that they had a new sentencing option, that of education of the principals in getting along in society without violence. Relevant statistics on violence case disposition need to be regularly disclosed. The percentage of training for the justice system participants needs to be equitable to violence cases they handle. The judicial system needs to facilitate the transfer of information regarding aggressors, their aggression, and their victims to appropriate agencies dealing with the recovery of the victims from the effects of the aggression.

The Health Care System

The health care system itself needs to develop and use safe and effective methods for identification of violence. Nurses and other practitioners can be trained in the use of the ultimate question with their patients. The system needs to provide referral, education, and support services to victims and their children. It needs to educate the aggressors on different methods of dealing with frustration and refrain from overly prescribing sedative drugs to aggressors and their victims to medicate their behavior. The health care system needs to use accountable documentation and reporting protocols for family aggression and to devote a percentage of training equitable to violence cases they handle. It needs to take responsibility for public health remedies instead of relying on medicine to solve all violence problems.

Government

The government needs to pass laws that define physical aggression in all forms as criminal behavior, *without exception*; vigorously and progressively make battering behavior illegal; create accountable standards for batterer-intervention programs; and require coordinated systems of intervention in family aggression. The government needs to provide ample funding to accomplish the goal of eradicating family aggression such as funding for battered women's service agencies and violence-prevention education for youth. Taxation is one way of generating incentives for the funding of programs dealing with family and community aggression. The government needs to pass laws that allow for the safe and easy transfer of information between governmental agencies that deal with aggressors, their aggression, and their victims.

Federal agencies need to act as leaders and facilitators, promoting shared responsibility for change at the federal, state, and local levels, and in the private sector, in such areas as public education, research, service system capacity, and technology development. States and communities, however, need to be the very center for system transformation; many have already begun this critical work. Their leadership in planning, financing, service delivery, and evaluation of consumer and family-driven services will significantly advance the transformation agenda. Finally, an emphasis on individual recovery and resilience will transform not only service delivery systems, but also hearts, minds, and lives for future generations. The emphasis of the governmental efforts needs to be on mental health, as defined above, instead of mental illness, as in current programs (*Federal Mental Health Action Agenda*) by the U.S. Department of Health and Human Services (HHS).

Employers

Employers need to place conditions on the batterers' continuing employment, including the mandate to remain nonviolent. They need to intervene actively against stalking in the workplace and support, financially and otherwise, advocacy and service for battered men, women, and children. They need to continually educate and dialogue about violence issues through personnel services and safeguard battered employees' jobs and careers by providing flexible schedules, leaves of absence, and establishing enlightened personnel policies. Employers need to provide employment security to battered employees and to provide available resources to support and advocate for them. Even though employers are not mandated reporters, they need to report any violence that occurs or is reported to occur involving their employees.

Clergy

The clergy need to conduct outreach within their congregations and provide a safe environment for people to discuss their experiences regarding violence. They need to develop internal policies for responding to violence. The clergy must speak out against violence from the pulpit and organize multi-faith coalitions to educate the religious community. They need to interact with the existing family aggression intervention community and routinely assess for aggression in premarital and pastoral counseling. Seeking out and maintaining a learning and referral relationship with the family aggression coordinated community response system is very important to the clergy. The clergy must send a strong message and take a stance of opposing biblical or theological justification for aggression and domestic violence and they must reject patriarchal dominance as a preferred social pattern. They need to advocate educating children how to live in society without violence and other anti-social behavior.

Media

And finally, the media must take the role of educator and be the textbook for the community. It must present the facts of the epidemic of violence against men, women, and children. The media needs to prioritize safety, equal opportunity, and justice over profit, popularity, and advantage. The media must prioritize subject matter that celebrates peace and non-violence even if means less income. Media members must expose and condemn abuse, secrecy, chauvinism, and the privilege of one gender over the other. The media needs to cease the glorification of violence against men, women, and children and, instead, spotlight efforts that promote nonviolence. Media professionals need to devote an equitable proportion of their product to the needs of battered victims and, instead of glorifying violence, the media needs to provide education about the dynamics and consequences of violence. Labeling family aggression as *love gone sour, lover's quarrels, family spats,* etc., needs to stop. Portraying the batterer's excuses and lies as if they were the truth only perpetuates these falsehoods. For every freedom comes a responsibility. The media must take responsibility for its *freedom of the press.* Attacking those who are against violence is a lack of responsibility on the media's part.

The failure of the above nine elements of a community program to work with a single purpose is illustrated in Jeremy's story. It exemplifies many of the shortcomings of the current programs in use with children who learn aggression in the home and practice it both in the home and in the community. A program such as that described above could take an active role in the reduction of gang violence, domestic violence, criminal activity, and many of the other problems with which our society deals. If our society turns from a punishing society to a teaching society, then, in my opinion, much of the aggression and lawlessness in the society will be eliminated. We can create peace instead of aggression and war.

These concepts have been used at the Ventura School for Girls in California; Huntington Woods School in Wyoming, Mich.; and in the City of Corning, N.Y.

British Prime Minister Tony Blair has taken a proactive response to the aggressive and anti-social behavior of some of the youth in London, England. After a rampage by youth, Blair's Labor Party believes that antisocial behavior is the most important issue for Britons—even more pressing than the economy, global warming, and the war in Iraq. The government has defined antisocial behavior as any activity that causes or is likely to cause harassment, alarm, or distress. This includes anything from drunkenness or urination to neighbors refusing to turn down their stereos and teenagers hanging outside shops intimidating prospective patrons, to actual acts of aggression and violence encompassing serious crimes such as assault, robbery, and arson. John Daniszewski reports in the *Los Angeles Times* (Column One, Feb. 6, 2006) that Blair's plan includes evicting families who are so out of control that they terrorize their neighborhoods from their homes. Blair continues, "The families could be put temporarily into supervised accommodations to undergo a barrage of re-education. Parents would be shown how to raise their children, and young people would be trained to live in a society of rules." There are critics of this program, but most agree that something needs to be done and that no single agency can do it. All of the agencies involved with aggressive youth agree that respect for self and others is one of the elements missing from the youth's education and lifestyle. Blair said, "We need a radical new approach if we are to restore the liberty of the law-abiding citizen.... Freedom to be safe from fear has to come first.... The challenge is to create and, where needed, enforce a modern culture of respect which the majority of people want." Blair believes that respect has broken down and societal bonds that once served as a check on incorrect or abusive behavior have disappeared. In the same article, Bob Reitemeier, Children's Society in London, said, "There is absolutely no denial that there is behavior out there in that world that really is unacceptable and it is a real problem that we all have to deal with it."

The English government has recognized the problem and is attempting to do something about it. In addition, Ireland, Sweden, Austria, Denmark, Finland, Germany, Iceland, and Norway have banned smacking of children by parents. This ban has resulted in a reduction of child abuse to virtually zero, according to Canadian psychologist Dr. Joan Durrant (Collins, 2006). Here in the United States, we may have to work on the problem by starting at the local level, moving up to the state level, and finally, to the federal level. But I believe that change has to start somewhere or the Jeremys of our communities will continue to be ill served and will continue to be community problems when they become adults.

Launched in April 2001, the Global Initiative to End All Corporal Punishment of Children aims to speed the end of corporal punishment of children across the world. The initiative reports to UNICEF and the United Nations. The global concept of eliminating child abuse is reaching everyone. The Global Initiative aims to

- Form a strong alliance of human rights agencies, key individuals and non-governmental organizations against corporal punishment;

- Make corporal punishment of children visible by building a global map of its prevalence and legality, ensuring that children's views are heard and charting progress towards ending it;
- Lobby state governments systematically to ban all forms of corporal punishment and to develop public education programs;
- Provide detailed technical assistance to support states with these reforms.

The website (www.endcorporalpunishment.org) gives the following information on the initiative's beliefs and purpose.

> Corporal punishment of children breaches their fundamental human rights to respect for human dignity and physical integrity. Its legality in almost every state worldwide—in contrast to other forms of interpersonal violence—challenges the universal right to equal protection under the law.
>
> Despite the growing consensus that corporal punishment breaches children's fundamental human rights, most of the world's children are still subjected to legalized assaults by their parents and by other caregivers and teachers.
>
> In states in every continent there have been moves to end corporal punishment in schools and penal systems (for example, in recent years in Ethiopia, Korea, South Africa, Thailand, Trinidad and Tobago, and Zimbabwe) and the issue is on the political agenda in many other states.
>
> At least ten countries have abolished all corporal punishment of children and more have reforms under discussion.
>
> Instituting the necessary legal changes is not expensive: what is required in almost every state is the explicit and well-publicized removal of any defense that currently justifies physical assault of children, in order to ensure that children have equal protection

under the law. Promotion of positive discipline can be built into other health promotion, education, and early childhood development programs.

The imperative for removing adults' assumed rights to hit children is that of fundamental human rights. Research into the harmful physical and psychological effects of corporal punishment, into the relative significance of links with other forms of violence, in childhood and later life, add further compelling arguments for condemning and ending the practice, suggesting that it is an essential strategy for reducing all forms of violence, in childhood and later life.

There is some danger that in becoming too preoccupied with this absorbing research, people forget the human rights imperative for action now: we do not look into the effects of physical discipline on women, or on animals. It is enough that it breaches fundamental rights. Finding some positive short-or long-term effects of corporal punishment would not reduce the human rights imperative for banning it.

Children, for too long the silent victims of corporal punishment, are beginning to express their own views about it. The Convention on the Rights of the Child requires states to enable children to express their views freely on all matters affecting them, and to give their views due consideration. Hearing children's voices should help to speed the end of corporal punishment.

Bringing Happiness to Families

This section of this chapter addresses the interaction within the community for *we, the people,* the *health care system,* the *social service system,* the *clergy,* the *judicial system,* and the *educational system* that can assist in bringing happiness and peace to all of the families in the community. It is each person's responsibility to protect our most important segment, the children. These are the segments of the community that have direct contact with children.

The first step in bringing happiness to families in the community is learning to recognize the symptoms of child abuse. Although child abuse is divided into four types—physical abuse, neglect, sexual abuse, and emotional maltreatment—the types are more typically found in combination than alone. A physically abused child, for example is often emotionally maltreated as well, and a sexually abused child may also be neglected. Any child at any age may experience any of the types of child abuse. Children over age five are more likely to be physically abused and to suffer moderate injury than are children under age five. The younger children, however, are more likely to be seriously injured or killed when they are abused. (Westat, Inc., 1988) Children over five are in school and will be seen by teachers and other school personnel who are mandated reporters. This provides a safety net for them. Children under five are, therefore, more vulnerable to undetected abuse.

Recognizing Child Abuse

Experienced educators likely have seen all forms of child abuse at one time or another. They are alert to signs like these that may signal the presence of child abuse.

The Child

- Shows sudden changes in behavior or school performance;
- Has not received help for physical or medical problems brought to the parents' attention;
- Has learning problems that cannot be attributed to specific physical or psychological causes;

- Is always watchful, as though preparing for something bad to happen;
- Lacks adult supervision;
- Is overly compliant, an overachiever, or too responsible;
- Comes to school early, stays late, and does not want to go home.

The Parent

- Shows little concern for the child, rarely responding to the school's requests for information, for conferences, or for home visits;
- Denies the existence of—or blames the child for—the child's problems in school or at home;
- Asks the classroom teacher to use harsh physical discipline if the child misbehaves;
- Sees the child as entirely bad, worthless, or burdensome;
- Demands perfection or a level of physical or academic performance the child cannot achieve;
- Looks primarily to the child for care, love and belonging, and satisfaction of emotional needs.

The Parent and Child

- Rarely touch or look at each other;
- Consider their relationship entirely negative;
- State that they do not like each other.

None of these signs proves that child abuse is present in a family. Any of them may be found in any parent or child at one time or another. But when these signs appear repeatedly or in combination, they should cause the educator, relative, or neighbor to take a closer look at the situation and to consider the possibility of child abuse. That second look may reveal further signs of abuse, or signs of a particular kind of child abuse.

One of the things that school personnel need to remember is the level of vocabulary of the child. The word "beat" can mean to win or to hit hard. The word "whipping" can also mean a spanking that may be a legal form of physical punishment under limited conditions. So, care must be taken in reporting suspected child abuse.

Signs of Physical Abuse

Consider the possibility of physical abuse when the child:

- Has unexplained burns, bites, bruises, broken bones, or black eyes;
- Has fading bruises or other marks noticeable after an absence from school;
- Seems frightened of the parents and protests or cries when it is time to go home from school;
- Shrinks at the approach of adults;
- Reports injury by a parent or another adult caregiver.

Consider the possibility of physical abuse when the parent or other adult caregiver:

- Offers conflicting, unconvincing, or no explanation for the child's injury;
- Describes the child as *evil*, or in some other very negative way;
- Uses harsh physical discipline with the child;
- Has a history of abuse as a child.

Signs of Neglect

Consider the possibility of neglect when the child:

- Is frequently absent from school;

- Begs or steals food or money from classmates;
- Lacks needed medical or dental care, immunizations, or glasses;
- Is consistently dirty and has severe body odor;
- Lacks sufficient clothing for the weather;
- Abuses alcohol or other drugs;
- States there is no one at home to provide care.

Consider the possibility of neglect when the parent or other adult caregiver:

- Appears to be indifferent to the child;
- Seems apathetic or depressed;
- Behaves irrationally or in a bizarre manner;
- Is abusing alcohol or other drugs.

Signs of Sexual Abuse

Consider the possibility of sexual abuse when the child:

- Has difficulty walking or sitting;
- Suddenly refuses to change for physical education or to participate in physical activities;
- Demonstrates bizarre, sophisticated, or unusual sexual knowledge or behavior;
- Becomes pregnant or contracts a venereal disease, particularly if under age fourteen;
- Runs away;
- Reports sexual abuse by a parent or another adult caregiver.

Consider the possibility of sexual abuse when the parent or other adult caregiver:

- Is unduly protective of the child, severely limits the child's contact with other children, especially of the opposite sex;
- Is secretive and isolated;
- Describes marital difficulties involving family power struggles or sexual relations.

Signs of Emotional Maltreatment

Consider the possibility of emotional maltreatment when the child:

- Shows extremes in behavior, such as overly compliant or demanding behavior, extreme passivity or aggression;
- Is either inappropriately adult (parenting other children, for example) or inappropriately infantile (frequently rocking or head-banging, for example);
- Is delayed in physical or emotional development;
- Has talked about death or suicide or attempted suicide;
- Reports a lack of attachment to the parent;
- Often seems sad, tired, restless, or out of sorts;
- Spends a great deal of time alone;
- Seems to have low self-esteem;
- Has trouble getting along with family, friends, and peers;
- Has frequent outbursts of shouting, complaining, or crying;
- Has trouble performing or behaving in school;
- Shows sudden changes in eating patterns;
- Sleeps too much or not enough;
- Has trouble paying attention or concentrating on tasks like homework;
- Seems to have lost interest in hobbies like music or sports;
- Shows signs of using drugs and/or alcohol.

Consider the possibility of emotional maltreatment when the parent or other adult caregiver:

- Constantly blames, belittles, or berates the child;
- Is unconcerned about the child and refuses to consider offers of help for the child's school problems;
- Overtly rejects the child.

Although the majority of abused children in the United States are of school age, school staff is traditionally responsible for only about 16 percent of cases reported each year. (National Clearinghouse on Child Abuse and Neglect Information, 1992) The report "Teachers Confront Child Abuse: A National Survey of Teacher's Knowledge, Attitudes, and Beliefs," conducted by the National Center for Prosecution of Child Abuse, has identified a number of barriers to school reporting. These barriers include lack of sufficient knowledge on how to detect and report cases of child abuse and neglect; fear of legal ramifications for false allegations; fear of the consequences of child abuse reports; parental denial and disapproval of reports; interference in parent-child relationships and family privacy; lack of community or school support; and school board or principal disapproval. (Abrahams, etc., 1989)

In my opinion, this situation can only improve with change. Teachers can become more knowledgeable about child abuse, child neglect, and the procedures followed by child protective services. Schools and communities can support staff that report child abuse and neglect. And school boards and administrators can become partners in preventing abuse and neglect. These changes will aid in reducing child abuse in the community. Since the schools see the children every day and are exposed to their emotional state, they are in a unique position to confront child abuse and the fear that a child has when they are being raised in an angering home.

CHAPTER 4

Discussion

Much of the material in this discussion chapter centers on the relationship of the individual with others. As described in the previous chapter, the application of the principles of Choice Theory to the community at large will bring about a reduction of aggression, not only with the individual, but also for the community as a whole. Increased happiness within an individual and his or her family brings about an increased ability to deal with the frustrations experienced in their daily life in the community. When the community uses Choice Theory with its members, all aggression is decreased and violence between people can be eliminated.

The diagram below explains in Choice Theory terms how the brain works and why we behave as we do. It was adapted from a more comprehensive chart developed by Dr. William Glasser and presented in *Chart Talk* (2000). The explanation emphasizes how Choice Theory is used both to counsel and to manage people. This simplified chart is used as a shorthand reference for group members who are familiar with the elements of Choice Theory so they can put the discussion in perspective and relate it to the overall theory. Often, during group discussions, the group refers to the elements of the chart to obtain clarity in understanding the relationship of events to Choice Theory concepts.

Choice Theory – Why And How We Behave

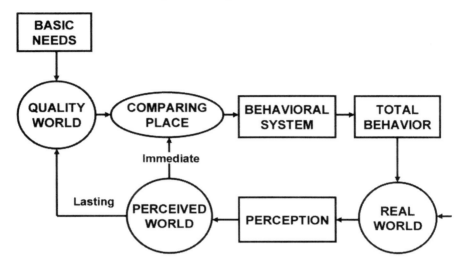

Reality Therapy, based on Choice Theory, is a unique counseling method. The following eight tenets explain Reality Therapy and are used in counseling aggressors.

1. People choose the total behavior that has led them into family aggression because it is their best effort to deal with a present, unsatisfying relationship.

2. The facilitator helps clients choose new relationship-improving behaviors that are more effective in satisfying one or more of their basic needs.

3. We must perceive that we have good relationships with other people to satisfy all of our basic needs. (The key to satisfying all five basic needs is satisfying the need for love and belonging while not giving up the need for power.)

4. Reality Therapy focuses on the here and now instead of on past events because love and belonging can only be satisfied in the present.

5. The solution to our problems is rarely found in discussions of the past unless the focus is on past successes and not failures.

6. Focusing on current symptoms avoids the real problem of improving present relationships.

7. The continuing goal of Reality Therapy is to create a Choice Theory relationship between the client and the facilitator as well as with the individuals in the group. The facilitator models the relationship with the client and thus sets an example of how it is accomplished.

8. Understanding and practicing Choice Theory is an integral part of practicing Reality Therapy. The clients are encouraged to integrate Choice Theory into their lives and relationships.

Reality Therapy gets to the root of the actual problem—improving present relationships or finding new ones that are more satisfying. The family is a logical starting point for improving the relationships. Diagnostic labels, brain drugs, and dreams are not used in Reality Therapy. People with conditions of mental illness, such as Alzheimer's disease, epilepsy, head trauma and brain infections, as well as genetic defects, such as Down's syndrome, Huntington's chorea, and autism should be treated primarily by neurologists instead of counselors or facilitators. Glasser does not label people as having a mental illness unless there is pathology in the brain. *Psychiatric symptoms are a person's current best attempt to regain inner control and emotional balance.*

Amond's Story

Dr. Amond is a medical doctor who was sentenced to the domestic class for disturbing the peace because he admitted to the judge that he and his fiancée had shouted at each other during their arguments. His fiancée accused him of hitting her in the mouth. Dr. Amond decided to go to trial and present evidence that he had not been violent with his fiancée. The judge determined that the fiancée was lying but sentenced Dr.

Amond to domestic violence classes for disturbing the peace because of the argument between Dr. Amond and his fiancée. Dr. Amond resigned himself to attending the classes and decided to get the most out of them. When I introduced the concept that brain drugs were not a part of Choice Theory, he took exception to it and questioned me. I suggested that he read Glasser's book, *Warning: Psychiatry Can Be Hazardous to Your Mental Health,* and gave him a copy.

Dr. Amond read the book and reported in class that it made some very valid points and that he was re-thinking his position. Medicine may be helpful in the beginning treatment of some of the behaviors associated with unhappiness, but in the long term, regaining one's happiness is not necessarily dependent on the continued use of drugs. Dr. Amond asked his mother, who was a teacher, to read the book and she supported his conclusions. He then asked his sister, who is a psychiatrist, to read the book. She said she was very familiar with Dr. Glasser's work and agreed with him that brain drugs were not necessary when treating the unhappiness caused by poor relationships.

Dr. Amond reports that since his investigation into the subject, he has reduced the prescribing of brain drugs by 70 percent with no noticeable adverse effects on his patients. He admits that some of his colleagues prescribe medication so their patients will become dependent upon them for the prescription renewal appointments that provide a continuing income.

Many clients come to the groups choosing to depress or to anger, and many of those are treated with medication. These clients are discovering that when they begin to make healthier choices in dealing with the problems in their lives, the medication is no longer needed. In addition, their families benefit from the return of happiness and energy to their home.

Total Behavior

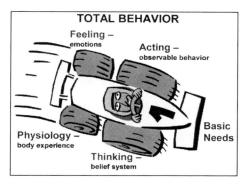

TOTAL BEHAVIOR
Feeling –
emotions
Acting –
observable behavior
Physiology –
body experience
Basic
Needs
Thinking –
belief system

Dr. Glasser defines all behavior as total behavior. Choice Theory explains that all behavior is composed of four distinct yet inseparable components: *acting, thinking, feeling,* and the *physiology* that accompanies the other three. That is why it is called *total behavior* instead of simply *behavior.* When our total behavior resembles someone else's behavior the Diagnostic and Statistics Manual of Mental Disorders (Fourth Ed.) categorizes, groups, and labels it. The labeling is used by insurance companies to designate payments for their medical-model treatment reimbursements. The courts have done the same thing by calling a group of behaviors domestic violence or child abuse or family aggression or battery to a domestic partner in a domestic setting. Actions and thoughts are clearly cognitive behaviors, and if we wish to change our total behavior, we must change the way we act and think. When the actions and thoughts are changed, the way we feel about things, even our physical being, is also changed. When we solve a problem, our stress is reduced, we can sleep better, and as a result, we feel better. The physical symptoms associated with the problem have been changed and we just feel better. Thinking and acting are the elements of total behavior that we use to satisfy our basic needs because they are the only components we can directly control. None of us can wish the past away. All we can do is control our own present total behavior.

The aggressor's first step in dealing with family aggression events is to take responsibility for the choices made. These choices started with the frustration that was felt and resulted in violence as defined by the law. These choices involve all four of the elements of total behavior. Acting out the lack of situational control was the violent behavior and the thinking was, "I need to control this situation." The feeling was one of frustration because events were not going as the aggressor wanted and envisioned in his quality world. The physiology element was most likely present in the elevated heart rate, tense muscles, and faster breathing that go along with most aggressive actions.

In one discussion of total behavior, a group member questioned the statement that we always take the best choice of action at the time we make the choice. I explained that a few minutes later, the choice we made earlier may turn out to be a poor choice, but at the time we made it, we thought it was the best available action to make. When I stated, "No one intentionally makes a bad choice," the client agreed with the original statement about always making the best choice. It is difficult for the aggressor to see that use of force is a poor choice because it always has worked in the past. We always have a choice, but we don't always have what we consider good choices.

Through domestic violence and parenting classes, clients begin to see how they can make better choices. They begin to practice making better choices in their lives. Clients begin to learn that they have other choices than the use of violence. As they learn about Choice Theory and their possible choices, their behavioral system expands to include many of these different choices.

Juan's Story

Juan was ordered by the judge to attend domestic violence class for being violent with his wife. While attending the group, he reported that he saw neighbors fighting. The husband was beating up his wife in the common area of the apartments. Juan stated that he got dressed and went outside to break up the fight. By the time he got there, the wife was bloody, lying on the ground, and the husband was still hitting her. Juan reported that he stepped between the two with his arms folded over his chest so as not to become a fighter himself. Juan just stayed between the two until the police arrived. The man hit Juan several times as he attempted to continue the fight with his wife. The responding police team consisted of a lead female officer and a male supporting officer. The male officer's questioning revealed that all parties reported that Juan had stepped between the husband and wife to break up the fight and was not a party to the fight himself. The male officer told this to the female officer. The female officer asked Juan if he was on probation and Juan answered truthfully that he was. The female officer checked his record and found that he had been convicted of domestic violence in the past and then she made the decision to take Juan to the station along with the other two people. Juan spent two nights in jail before going before a judge. After hearing the story from all three, the judge determined that Juan had not committed any crime, but instead was trying to protect the woman. The judge released Juan immediately.

After additional deliberation, Juan stated that he was responding to a principle in his quality world that stated that it was not correct for a man to hit a woman. He perceived that he could intervene and stop this injustice. He stated that he was anxious and that his heart was racing. He said that his total behavior was "reacting to the situation in the same old way" without thinking about the elements and consequences. The reactions were based on his past learning in his behavioral system. He did not think much about the situation before acting. Juan came to the conclusion that calling 911 on his cell phone or his cordless phone while he was walking toward the couple might have been a better choice. This would have provided some witness to his story. Calling 911 would have provided contact with the police prior to their arrival, and would have established his intentions and actions before his previous domestic violence arrest became an overriding factor. In intervening and protecting the woman, Juan was imposing external control on the situation instead of giving the couple its own choice as to behavior. Juan continued to think that protecting the woman was the proper thing to do to make his perceived world consistent with his quality world.

Further review of the incident might include asking some additional questions. Whom was Juan trying to control and why was he trying to control the situation? What in his quality world was driving his desire to control the situation? What was his total behavior before he made the choice to intervene? What were his actions, feelings, physiology, and thoughts? Did the past behavioral system drive the feelings, physiology, and actions, minimizing the thinking element? What other actions might have kept Juan from being taken to jail while still satisfying his basic needs and quality world? How could he participate in the situation without trying to control others by external means? If someone's life is in jeopardy—is external control ok? How would the situation look to the police officers when they arrived and conducted the limited investigation? What did he perceive in the real world that put his comparison between his perceived world and his quality world so out of balance that he thought it required the intervention?

Relationship

The second step in dealing with the client and his or her partner and children is the relationship. The relationship must be evaluated if it is to continue as a caring and happy one. The aggressive act might have been the terminating incident and the parties are going to separate. If there are children, the problem involves more than the two partners. If this continuing relationship is one of aggression, there will be long-lasting psychological problems. These problems will always be a part of the family's present lives. The happiness of the family is dependent upon the happiness of each of its members.

One reason for continuing in a relationship, even a violent one, is that one or more of the parties believes the relationship can make feelings of loneliness go away. Many of us have tried to find a way to outwit or escape our own loneliness, but we have learned that we cannot outwit our loneliness without satisfying our need for love and belonging. As fathers look at their children, they may wish to spare them this pain. As men and women with partners, they have dreamed of a quality world where all loneliness was dispelled.

We cannot obliterate loneliness. But we can learn to accept and deal with it. There is no need to be compulsive about covering all traces and all reminders that we are alone. We can accept this universal truth. We are alone and solely responsible for our choices and chosen total behavior, but so is everybody else. We can make true contact with each other out of our aloneness. True intimacy with another person comes out of first seeing our separateness, and then bridging the gap by using the caring habits. Many of us have felt so much pain in our relationships that we often feel lonely. Or we may have been so frightened of being alone that now we avoid it like poison. All of us have known the pain of loneliness, even while we were surrounded by people.

Loneliness and solitude are very different feelings. When we feel lonely, we feel sad about being alone. But when we experience solitude, we have ourselves and can be at peace. Our quality world and our perceived world are in harmony and our love and belonging need is satisfied.

When experiencing solitude, we can become more fully acquainted with ourselves, develop greater honesty, and deepen our internal power. Even in our solitude, we are not alone.

As family aggression groups deal only with the aggressor, the description of the ongoing relationship is a one-sided opinion. Only time in the group will reveal the reality of this opinion. As explained in Appendix A, the client is the only reporter of what is wrong with the relationship. Usually the client starts out using external control by saying he was aggressive because the partner made him aggressive; he was only trying to get away from the fight. The Choice Theory education process begins with this report of the incident. Most of the time, the other members of the group who have learned about Choice Theory confront the new member by asking if the partner or child controls the client or if the client controls the partner or child. They then explain to the new client that they control themselves and that they cannot control their partners and children, nor can the partners and children control them. Therefore, the client is responsible for choosing to act aggressively. It will take several sessions for new clients to start to understand this principle, and even more time for them to accept it for themselves. The groups are segregated by sex and are not combined in any manner. The experience of teaching both men's and women's groups has shown me that both men and women have the same issues with anger and aggression, but they express their anger differently in most cases.

In the groups, I ask a new client to explain why he stayed with his partner. What is good about the relationship right now? Much of the time, the only answer is the sex. Another often-used answer is that he stays because of the child or children. Other people think they are special because their wife is a "real babe" or that they are "a real stud." Seldom does the client state that he is still in love with his partner and that he wants to change his life to make the relationship work better. Some say that they are willing to change their way of relating to others, like Lute in Appendix A, but most of the clients say that they are not willing to change first. They say, "Why do I have to do all of the changing and she does not have to do any? It is not fair." When the clients say that something is not *fair*, I respond that *fair* only occurs in Pomona, a town near Los Angeles that hosts the annual county fair. *Fair* is a matter of opinion and depends on who is making the judgment. Life is not fair; it just is. It is left to us to choose how we will respond. This group is designed to help them learn how to live a life of better choices and not to even things out for their poor choices. Only they can be in charge of their own choices. *Fairness* does not play a part in learning how to make better choices in life.

The clients do not know what they can do to make their relationships better. They think that all they have to do is find the *right partner*—one who will behave in the manner that they want and treat them the way they want to be treated—while they continue with their present behavior. Most clients are afraid that their existing partner or a new partner will report them to the police for *false* charges of aggression against them or their children. They view this fear as external control. They think that once they have a record, the police or children's services will arrest them or take their children without listening to them. This is often true. Sometimes the police give the female partners the advantage by arresting the male without doing a thorough investigation. This is especially true if the male has a previous record of family aggression. The client has to learn that in selecting a new partner, he should look for one who uses Choice Theory in her own life. If she does, then they both stand a great chance of having a satisfying relationship and he can be free from the fear of being reported for false charges. He can still be a caring parent to his children from the past relationship. Henry's story illustrates how a parent can be caring with his children even though the relationship with their mother is not very good. Without Choice Theory, the relationship suffers from the constant effort to force the partner and children to be different or to punish each other for the wrongs, real or perceived, which cause most of the problems. This external control poisons every relationship in which it is used.

Henry's Story

Henry reported using Choice Theory with his twelve year old son, Charles, after reading some of Dr. Glasser's books. Henry is separated from his wife due to physical aggression in their relationship. One day when Henry had custody of his children, they went to Denny's for dinner. Charles was projecting an attitude and was causing trouble for everyone at the restaurant. Henry told his son that if he chose to continue the attitude and disruptive behavior, he did not want Charles to come on the upcoming weekend's visit. Charles quieted for the remainder of the meal. Henry and his children went shopping and while they were walking around in the store, Charles remained distant from the rest of the group. After a while, Charles began getting closer and closer to the group. Finally, Henry asked him if he had anything to say about his behavior. This moved Charles farther away from the group. He continued his attitude for the rest of the evening until he and his siblings returned to their mother's home. Charles was struggling with his need for love and belonging and his need for power. The two were in conflict with each other.

The next day, Charles' mother called Henry, confronted him about the situation, and tried to intercede for their son. Henry maintained that he wanted to talk with Charles about the situation and his behavior and not discuss it through a third party. The mother and Henry concluded the phone call without Charles getting on the phone, but she understood that their son needed to talk with his father before he was welcome back into Henry's home. The next day Charles called and apologized for his behavior and was promptly welcomed on the next visit along with his siblings. Henry explained that he was uncomfortable being around Charles when Charles acted up the way he had done in Denny's and that their relationship was strained when Charles acted out.

Henry told the group that after reading the books, he realized that the relationship he had with his son was more important than punishing Charles, using external control, for acting up in the restaurant. This was the method that Henry chose—to use the strength of the relationship to provide information to Charles about proper behavior toward others and to let him choose behavior that would strengthen the bonding between them. Henry chose to support the need for love and belonging that each of them had and thus strengthen the relationship between them.

A few weeks later, the children were visiting Henry again and this time they wanted to watch TV and play games on the TV. Henry had planned an outing for the family, but the children did not want to stop playing and chose not to get ready. Henry asked them several times, but then realized that his asking sounded like one of the seven deadly habits, nagging, and he stopped. He retired into his bedroom to be by himself for a while and think about the most effective total behavior to maintain a pleasant relationship with his children. He decided to wait until a TV program that he wanted to watch came on and then he went into the living room and switched the TV to his football game. He told the children that they had their time with the TV and now it was his turn.

When the children could not have their way, they wanted to go on the family outing. It was too late and so Henry declined and continued to watch his football game. When the children complained, Henry asked if their mother let them do anything they wanted whenever they wanted. The children responded that she did and Henry answered with his expectations of the children when they were with him. Henry said that when a family outing was planned, he expected the children to consider the short time that they were with their father. If all of them were to have a weekend that satisfied all of their needs, each member of the family would have to consider the other members in his or her decisions and total behavior. Henry was starting to teach Choice Theory to his children. His children went home and told their mother what Henry had done—not letting them watch TV and then not going on the outing. Their mother informed her lawyer just how poorly Henry was treating the children and how bad a parent Henry had been. When the mother's lawyer contacted Henry's lawyer and Henry's lawyer contacted Henry, Henry reminded his lawyer that he was the one who had completed the parenting class. The mother had not taken any parenting classes as recommended by the Department of Children and Family Services. He also informed his lawyer that he was using a well-established psychological theory, Choice Theory, to strengthen the relationship with his children. He also stated that this was used in his domestic violence class. As the children's visits with their father continued, their relationship with their father became much stronger because they learned that they could talk about how each person's behavior affected the feelings of the rest of them and they could discuss their interrelationships without being told that they were wrong.

Henry was also able to apply Choice Theory to his youngest son, Jimmy, when Jimmy started a fire in his mother's garage by playing with her lighter. Jimmy lit a cardboard box and then put the fire out by hitting the fire with a book until it went out. Henry took the children to a firehouse, the same one that his parents had taken him to when he was Jimmy's age, and asked if anyone could talk with Jimmy about fires. The captain came out and took Jimmy and Henry into his office where they talked about fires and the captain showed them some pictures of burns. Henry's other two children were treated to a show of the fire engines and equipment while the captain was talking with Jimmy and Henry. After the talk ended, the firefighters showed Jimmy and Henry the fire engines and equipment, too. This turned out to be a fun learning experience for the children. This is how Henry chose to deal with Jimmy's normal acting out by teaching him something, instead of punishing him for setting a fire.

Frustration and Anger

When a client brings anger and misery into the group, it stops all therapeutic endeavors and can be contagious. If a client refuses to dissipate his anger and continues to spew it out in the group, he is asked to leave for the day or find another group. This program is for those who want to improve their lives, not for individuals who continue to use anger to force others to obey them. Frustration is an oft-occurring feeling when things do not happen to satisfy the basic needs and match the images of the quality world. The clients in family aggression groups have let that frustration build into anger and then to rage and violence by not dealing with it as it occurs. Frustration occurs when we experience powerlessness to control our immediate environment and thus our basic power need is not satisfied. The client needs to learn the total behavior that will deal with the feeling of frustration and satisfy the basic need of power in a positive manner instead of using the learned behavior that brought the courts into his real world.

The group members learn a combination of concepts. They learn that Choice Theory can be used to deal with the frustration of life's situations and that the equality of partners in the relationship is most important, replacing the external power and control that has characterized the relationship in the past. They also learn techniques that can be used to release the tension of anger in safe and peaceful ways.

One of the concepts discussed in the group is that the relationship is more important than either person is. If the ego of either of the partners is so great as to be supreme, the relationship does not stand much chance of success. One way to resolve disagreements is the solving circle. After a time-out where both parties can calm down and regain their cognitive control, they can then sit down and discuss the problem. If they envision a circle around them and picture their relationship in this circle with them, they can both discuss what they can do to make the relationship better instead of satisfying their individual egos. The solving circle can be used parent to parent, parent to child, and child to child. Glasser states that an important element of the solving circle is one of the concepts of Choice Theory:

> Never do anything or say anything in the relationship that experience tells you will move you farther apart from your partner (or child).

There are four steps to the solving circle and this concept is paramount in its use.

1. When they enter the circle, the parties are agreeing that the relationship takes precedence over what each of them wants as an individual.

2. When the parties step into the solving circle, they agree to use the caring habits. No matter how serious the disagreement, they must stay in the circle and negotiate the difference.

3. If no compromise can be reached in the first attempt, one or more must be willing to say, "What I want right now is more important to me than this relationship. I am going to step out of the circle now, but I am willing to try again tomorrow."

4. The next time the parties get into the circle they should be willing to say, "It is more important that we stay in this circle than that we want as an individual."

The total behaviors that will move a person farther from his or her partner are the seven deadly habits. These seven deadly habits will get in the way of a positive relationship and bring frustration and anger into the relationship. These habits are the external control elements that push the partnership apart and can stretch the relationship to the breaking point. When I ask the clients, "Who wants to be with someone who criticizes them all the time?" the answer is always, "Not me!" The same goes with blaming, complaining, nagging, threatening, punishing, and bribing. If there are children in the union, the client can see this much more easily in their lack of response to the parent's directives. Use of external control will usually drive partners and children apart because no one wants to be someone else's puppet.

Choice Theory suggests that the partners and children can bring about a positive relationship by using the seven caring habits. These habits bring people closer together and answer the ultimate question in the affirmative.

Terry's Story

Terry was also in the group for being violent with his wife, who is addicted to methamphetamine and alcohol. After an investigation of the home to determine the safety of their child, the Department of Children and Family Services arranged for Terry and his wife to sign an agreement stating that Terry would move out of the house until his wife entered a drug rehabilitation facility. The Family Law Court gave Terry custody of his child and ordered his wife to have a monitor for her visits with the child. The court gave Terry authority to choose the monitor and he decided to trust the parents of the wife (his in-laws) to provide safety for his child when the child visits with the mother. Terry agreed to obtain a restraining order against his wife so that she could not come near him or his home. On one Sunday visit, Terry went to pick up the child at the maternal grandparent's home. Mother was at the house in violation of the restraining order and she would not let Terry leave with the child. Mother kept blocking the path between Terry and his car. She pushed and hit Terry while he was holding the child. This put the child at risk of physical abuse. Terry decided to call 911 to have the police assist him in getting away from the grandparents' home. When the police arrived, they assessed the situation and talked with Terry, the mother, and her parents. The grandparents told the police that Terry was preventing the mother from leaving, that Terry was the aggressor in the family, and that he should be jailed for his repeat offences of domestic violence. The police took Terry to jail and booked him on spousal abuse charges. Terry spent the night in jail. The next day Terry paid a $2,000 bail bond and was released. When Terry went to court, the district attorney declined to prosecute the case because the restraining order allowed Terry to have contact with the mother while they were exchanging the child and there was no evidence of violence toward the mother.

Terry stated in group that before he had been introduced to Choice Theory, he would have put the child down and forced the mother out of the way by pushing her to the ground or hitting her. He then would have picked up his son, gotten into his car, and left. As a result of attending the groups, Terry thought about alternative actions and called the police.

After this incident, Terry decided to stop using the maternal grandparents as monitors for the mother's visits with the child. He was staying at his sister's home and she agreed to monitor the visits. A few weeks later, Terry called the maternal grandparents to inform them and the mother that he planned to take the child camping over the weekend. If the mother wanted to visit with the child, she would have to visit on Thursday evening. The mother came over without notifying anyone or obtaining permission from Terry's sister to come into her home. The mother knocked on the door and when Terry opened it with the child in his arms, the mother was standing there, smelling of alcohol. She started yelling at Terry and threw something at him. Terry turned around to close the door and she socked him in the head as he was going back into the house. Terry thought twice about calling the police this time because of the last incident. He decided to call them the next day after things had cooled down.

The next day, even though Terry was hesitant, he called the police to document the incident as a violation of the restraining order. The same police officers came to his home and found a lump on his head where his wife had hit him. They took his statement and made an appointment to return the following day to take the statement from Terry's sister. On the following day, Saturday, the police took the statement of Terry's sister and decided to file felony charges of domestic violence and violation of the restraining orders against Terry's wife. While they were taking the testimony, Terry's wife was at her parents' home where she got into an altercation with her parents. Police were called again to the grandparents' home. The two teams of police officers communicated from home to home and the officers at Terry's residence heard the yelling and screaming of Terry's wife at the grandparent's home. Terry's wife seemed to be out of control and threatened suicide. The police at the grandparents' home evaluated Terry's wife as being a danger to herself and she was committed to a hospital.

In class, Terry went through the Choice Theory diagram above and stated that he had changed his way of behaving because of the group and his understanding of Choice Theory. He said that his behavior system had changed from instant reaction with force to thinking about the ultimate desired gain. This led him to a more rational total behavior to obtain his desired outcome. He said the first incident had made him wary of the police when both he and his wife were there because they may have a tendency to protect the woman over the man even if the woman is the aggressor. He also realized that he could not trust the grandparents to report the truth when their daughter was in the wrong. His perceptions of the real world changed the way he viewed the events of the second incident, and the changes were stored in his perceived world for future use and comparison with his quality world. Terry said his basic needs of freedom and love and belonging could be better met with his new perceptions of how he interacted in the real world. He replaced his old anger with the new perceptions and elevated the level of happiness in his life.

Clients are very creative with their total behavior. They create elaborate concepts to justify their behavior and choose just as elaborate behaviors to solve problems in meeting their basic needs. Anger and depressing are among the most common choices. Some choose drinking or drugs; some choose isolation from society; some choose anxiety; and some choose manic behavior along with the depressing behavior. Some choose listening to voices in their heads tell them what to do because they are so confused that they have given cognitive control of themselves to their inner voices.

Clients are creative in all that they do and say. Examples of creativity may be mimicking performances by actors, dancers, and athletes. When actors portray a character, they must take on all of that character's total behavior. The actor has to not only think and act as if he or she was the character, but he or she must have the feelings and physiology to make the portrayal of the character believable to the audience. If an actor would pretend to be sad and heartbroken over the loss of a child, then he or she must have the feeling inside and the tears coming from the eyes to complete the scene. Just saying that he or she is sad and heartbroken will not get the job done.

There is creative acting in all of the things that we do. Examples of each element of total behavior are the *action* when Michael Jordan scores a basket; the *thinking* in the solutions to problems that one faces; the *feelings* in the way one attacks a situation, as in the will to get ahead or win a game; and the *physiology* in the way some people have performed great feats to save someone's life. Every total behavior clients choose has a creative component. When they choose helpful creativity and reject destructive creativity, they make more peaceful choices of total behavior. The total behavior symptoms are created for the following three reasons:

1. The symptom helps the client restrain the energy of anger that is always present whenever the client is frustrated.
2. The symptom is a way of crying for help, because people want to avoid an angry person.
3. The client uses symptoms to avoid situations they fear will increase the frustration.

Many clients mask their anger and call for help by creating physical symptoms. If both clients and the doctors who treat them could learn that frustration is the underlying cause of most ailments and that the client is able to create most any action, thought, feeling, or physiology his or her brain is capable of experiencing, they could save considerable time and effort by treating the root cause, frustration.

Basic Needs

The quality world is the dream life that satisfies the basic generic needs. It is the personal Shangri-La, the White Picket Fence dream life, or the ideal way we picture ourselves in the world around us. Glasser describes the five basic needs as *survival, love and belonging, power, freedom,* and *fun.* We build our quality world such that it satisfies our basic needs. The quality world is the core of our lives because it motivates us to consider the total behavior that we believe will satisfy our basic needs. This tight feedback loop is constantly being compared with the real world and events around us. This is the process by which we make choices to bring ourselves into peaceful stability. We constantly try to create situations that will satisfy our basic needs because we cannot satisfy the needs directly. Health and happiness come from meeting our basic needs through involvement with others.

During group sessions, I ask clients to establish the levels of their basic needs by looking at their past actions and desires as a starting reference from which to develop a description of their quality world. The clients look at others in the world to compare their need levels. They look at political leaders, successful business personalities, and sports figures for examples of power. They look at celebrities or heroes for examples of survival and fun. They look at other lifestyles for examples of freedom. Moreover, they look at their relationships and the connected relationships of others for examples of love and belonging. Love and belonging is a measure of their loving and cooperating with other people. Power is a measure of their competing, achieving, and gaining importance. The power we speak about is not external power, but the power over ourselves and the belief that we are in control of our beliefs and total behavior. This power is often called self-esteem, self-worth, or internal value. External power does not satisfy our need for power, but only leads to the desire for more external power. Freedom is a measure of mobility and desire to make choices for themselves. I explain that fun is not only playing, but it is learning as well. Most of the clients agree that the groups are fun once they are learning how to change their lives toward more peaceful decisions. At times, there is a great deal of laughter in the groups. Many times this laughter is generated by the actions of others that look ridiculous in light of the outcomes they generated. A client may think that an action was the best thing he could do at the time, but looking back at the action makes it seem funny and totally improper for the desired outcome. Finally, survival is a measure not only of the desire to remain alive and healthy, but also of the desire to have children and be a parent. After establishing the levels of their basic needs, they look at their quality world by listing those persons, places, things, and beliefs that are important to them. This is just a starting list; as their time with the group continues, they constantly review these elements and move them around as to importance and the interrelationship between them. They begin to see that it is often the conflict between these elements that leads to their discomfort and they can then start to get more information about them. They then make better choices to reduce the pain that leads to the frustration. These better choices lead to total behaviors that satisfy the frustration and basic needs. When clients make painful or difficult-to-understand choices, it is not because they enjoy them. It is because they do not know anything better to do. By bringing the elements out in the open for discussion of other choices, they are able to make choices that will better satisfy their basic needs.

It is my job, as the facilitator, to guide the clients in actually starting to do something about their problems. This effort is the key factor in the success of Reality Therapy using Choice Theory. Since these clients have lived lives that are steeped in external-control thinking, the use of force to get what they want, and control by others and society, the primary task is to influence them to rid themselves of external-control thinking. The clients can then realize that equality in a relationship will lead to a more peaceful relationship and the satisfaction of their basic needs.

Many clients focus on the problems of the past and the wrongs that others have done to them. This focus must be turned to the present because that is the only place where the actions and thoughts can take place. Total behavior is in the here and now. The lessons the clients learn are from these past actions, but the changed behavior is in the here and now. It is the present life situation that the client is trying to change. Most clients are court ordered and must deal with demands such as attending group every week, having progress reports sent to court and/or Children's Services, other court orders, and the money it takes to pay for the court-ordered services. Additionally, clients must deal with people involved in the family aggression who are not very pleased about the situation. Clients have enough to deal with in the present; therefore, to have them try to make plans at the beginning of their experience during group would not be productive. Once their lives have been stabilized, there will be plenty of time to deal with future activities. If they choose to end the relationship that existed when they were violent, future activities might include choosing a new partner. My goal is to have clients base their new relationships on the compatibility of their new partner as a result of what they have learned from the group and Choice Theory.

There are a number of red flags that represent personality differences between the client and a potential mate. The meanings of red flags are discussed in the group. The discussion starts with, "Is your relationship bad for your health or heading into dangerous territory?" I ask the clients to take this test to find out. If they answer yes to more than two of the categories, I recommend they turn to someone for help. These red flags represent difficulties that can come from either partner.

Is he or she someone who …

- Is jealous and possessive toward you, will not let you have friends, checks up on you, and will not accept breaking up?

- Tries to control you by being very bossy, giving orders, making all the decisions, or not taking your opinion seriously?

- Is scary? Do you worry about how this person will react to things you say or do? Does this person threaten you, use or own weapons, or threaten with kitchen tools?

- Is violent? Does this person have a history of fighting; losing his or her temper, or bragging about mistreating or dominating others? Has hit, pushed, choked, restrained, kicked, or physically abused you?

- Pressures you for sex, is forceful or scary about sex? Attempts to manipulate or guilt-trip you by saying, "If you really loved me, you would ..." or gets too serious about the relationship too fast for comfort?

- Abuses drugs or alcohol and pressures you to take them?

- Blames you when you are mistreated? Says you provoked it?

- Has a history of bad relationships, and blames the other person for all the problems?

- Believes that he or she should be in control and powerful and that you should be passive and submissive?

- Makes your family and friends concerned about your safety?

- Has no friends or his friends are violent toward others?

- Dismisses your opinions?

- Has broken the law and been jailed?

- Seems to be too good to be true?

- Says, "Only call me on my cell."

- Says, "I've never had a true friend until I met you."

- Says, "I called you many times and you didn't answer."

One of the concepts clients learn is that by knowing the levels of their own basic needs, they can chose a more compatible partner by taking the time to get to know the levels of their new partner's basic needs. A series of questions given in Chapter Eight can assist clients in determining the level of their basic needs. This compatibility match will minimize many of the difficulties that may arise in the future.

Al's Story

Al contends that his wife falsely accused him of hitting her. He is now in the process of finalizing the custody arrangements of their two children. He had full custody of them for the past few years, but when he wanted to move back to his hometown in the East, he made a temporary agreement for their mother to have custody until he found a permanent situation. Once settled, he planned to return to California to move the children to his new home. The move did not work out because he could not be licensed due to his conviction for domestic violence in California. When Al came back to California, the children's mother would not return the children to him.

Al knew about Choice Theory because of his participation in the domestic violence group. He decided to use it as a way of living and apply it to his choice of behavior. During one group session, Al explained how he applied the concepts of Choice Theory to a discussion he had with his current girlfriend. He described how she was using the seven deadly habits in her attack on him for the way he was handling his ex-wife and the custody of the children. He repeated several of the remarks that his girlfriend had used and concluded by citing one particularly hurtful criticism. He realized that if his girlfriend could hit below the belt in that manner, she was someone he did not want in his quality world. This was a red flag for him. He thought about it for a short while and walked away from the relationship.

I asked Al how the event illustrated the use of Choice Theory in his life. He said that his girlfriend was not meeting his basic need of love and belonging. She communicated with him in a manner that did not match the picture of the ideal mate in his quality world. In the real world, his girlfriend criticized, complained, and blamed him in her description of what he should have done with his ex-wife. This hurt him deeply. Not only did she use the seven deadly habits at this time, but he also realized that this was her normal communication style. His perception of her changed from the ideal mate to a person who could and would hurt him deeply. When he compared his girlfriend to his ideal mate in his quality world, he realized that this girlfriend was not a match and that his life was out of balance. His old behavior system would have had him react to the hurt with anger, trying to return the hurt to her. He realized that he had three choices—accept her as she is, leave her and move on to another relationship, or change his quality world image of a partner. After accepting Choice Theory as a way of life, he thought about an appropriate response and walked away from the relationship calmly. His total behavior was new and different from what he had chosen in the past and he was pleased with his progress and remained happy with the decision.

A few weeks later, his girlfriend called him to say that she had read the book *Getting Together and Staying Together,* by William and Carleen Glasser. The call came as a complete surprise to Al because he had not made any conditions on their separation. She knew he believed in Choice Theory and that he had read the book and chosen to live by its concepts. She said that she wanted to change and have a relationship with Al like the ones described in the book. The new information from his girlfriend led Al to decide to try the relationship again. In evaluating his total behavior and quality world, he found that he was not willing to change his quality world image of a partner, but he was willing to give her another chance to be that mate because he still had feelings for her.

Addictive Clients

Alcohol consumption reduces the ability of an individual to make cognitive decisions that restrain the individual from acting out in an antisocial manner. This does not mean that the person is an alcoholic; he or she may just be a social drinker. Abundant documentation illustrates this point, giving examples of people who get into situations after consuming alcohol or other drugs that place them in physical danger, social disgrace, or at odds with the people with whom they are in a relationship. For example, husbands who binge drink are three times more likely to abuse their wives than husbands who abstain (Kaufman-Kantor and Straus, 1987). Kaufman-Kantor and Straus concluded that a causal relationship between alcohol and family aggression has not been proven because 80 percent of the binge drinkers did not abuse their wives. Instead, alcohol abuse may result from, or be related to, other stresses that increase the chance of violence. However, the researchers found that socioeconomic factors and perceived norms regarding approval of violence were associated with spousal abuse, independent of alcohol use. In 60 to 75 percent of families where a woman is battered, her children are battered as well. Partner abuse survivors may also use alcohol as a coping mechanism (Kaufman-Kantor and Asdigian, 1997a). What can the children use to cope with the aggression in the home? Can this be the reason that drug and alcohol abuse is on the rise with teens?

Substance use and abuse often coexist with anger and violence. Data from the Substance Abuse and Mental Health Services Administration's National Household Survey on Drug Abuse, for example, indicated that 40 percent of frequent cocaine users reported engaging in some form of violent behavior. Anger and violence often can have a causal role in the initiation of drug and alcohol use and can also be a consequence associated with substance abuse. Individuals who experience traumatic events, for example, often experience anger and act violently, as well as abuse drugs or alcohol.

Clinicians often see how anger and violence are linked to substance abuse. One way they are linked is in the thinking of the client. Many substance abuse and mental health clients are victims of traumatic life events, which, in turn, lead to substance use, anger, and violence. Since violence often results in a criminal event and since many of the clients are also users of drugs and alcohol, the thinking about these two issues are often combined or linked together. Both the criminal and the addict use short-term thinking that results, most times, in long term pain—imprisonment or institutionalization or death. Addictive thinking patterns are common to all addicts, though not every addict has every single one. Addictive thinking patterns say that continuing to use alcohol and other drugs is okay no matter what the consequences are. Addictive thinking overlaps greatly with criminal thinking and the two reinforce and drive each other. The thinking patterns of the addict and the criminal are listed below.

Addict Thinking	**Criminal Thinking**
• No long term goals	• No long term goals
• Self-pity	• Victim
• Only responsible for self	• Not responsible to or for others
• "I take what I want."	• "I take what I want."
• "Look at all of the good I've done."	• "I'm good and deserving."
• "I'm different, I won't get hooked."	• "No one is like me."
• Life centered on personal pleasure	• Exciting life
• Afraid of feelings and change	• Afraid of getting caught
• "How can I get some more?"	• "I want it now."
• Control with deceit	• Control with power
• Quick fix	• Quick money

Despite the connection of anger and violence to substance abuse, few treatments have been developed to address anger and violence problems among people who abuse substances. Clinicians have found the dearth of treatment approaches for this important issue disheartening because addicts change their goals to meet the needs of their addiction, where as non-addicts will change their behavior to meet their goals.

If the drug or addictive behavior is more important to the addict than the relationship, the relationship will suffer and may not last. The twelve-step program, Alanon, is designed to assist the non-addict in the relationship in dealing with the difficulties that arise when the addict practices his addiction. This program is also one of choice and responsibility, like Choice Theory. Alanon teaches that it is the partner's choice to stay in the relationship or leave it, but the partner cannot change the addict. It is the partner's responsibility to take care of him or her self and not to assist the addict in any manner with his addiction. Choice Theory concepts correspond with the concepts of twelve-step programs, but add more insight as to why and how people behave, the compatibility of partners, and the behaviors that separate partners and those that bring partners together. Choice Theory addresses happiness in addition to sobriety.

The belief that one has more power than they previously had is at the very heart of addiction, so much so that no mater how much power addicts may have, it is never enough. Addiction is the disease of *more*—the need for *more* of the stimulant and/or *more* often. To get that feeling of power, there is no price that addicts are unwilling to pay. They are willing to harm themselves by staying with their addiction for the chance to gain a sense of power that goes beyond admiration and respect. The addiction even extends to their belief that they have gained so much power that people are now afraid of what they may do. Freedom also plays a part in the addiction in the sense that the addict thinks that he or she is free to do what he or she wants with his or her own body. What the addict seems to lack is the belief that love is what they need. They are so into power that love and belonging have taken a back seat to the thirst for more power. To be cured of the addiction, the addict must make an effort both to give and to accept enough love and belonging to satisfy him or herself and to help satisfy someone else. Two-thirds of partner abuse victims (those abused by a current or former spouse, boyfriend, or girlfriend) reported that alcohol had been a factor. For the spouse abuse victims, the offender was drinking in three out of four cases. (Greenfield, 1998)

Violent incidents frequently involve alcohol use by the perpetrator, victim, or both. Alcohol use can increase the likelihood and severity of family aggression incidents. Kaufman-Kantor and Asdigian (1997b) also found that when men experience the alcohol-related physical sensations of arousal, such physiology includes increased heart rate and blood pressure. They may *misattribute* such physiology as increased aggression or dominance. Women are less likely to make such a connection, possibly because of socialization. According to Stets and Straus (1990), men underreport perpetrating partner abuse, and female aggression victims tend to sustain more severe injuries than male victims at a rate of about seven to one.

Leonard (1992) affirmed that a husband's drinking pattern in and of itself would not be predictive of marital violence; a motivation for aggression would also be necessary. Men with a high level of negative affect and those with high levels of hostility were more likely to have patterns of risky drinking and to abuse their wives and children. Men with low levels of hostility were more likely to abuse their wives and to engage in risky drinking if their level of marital satisfaction was low. A high level of alcohol involvement among men who scored low in anger and depression rankings leads to the speculation that alcohol acted to release control of suppressed anger.

Alcohol appears to be used more frequently in violent crimes between intimates than in violent crimes between acquaintances, strangers, or other relatives. (U. S. Department of Justice, 1998) I believe this is because we have more and closer history with our intimates and our desire to control their lives is greater than our desire to control the lives of others. With other people, we only want to control the current incident and not their entire lives

Many clients come to group because of actions taken while under the influence of legal or illegal drugs. Addicting drugs mimic or activate the pleasure-producing brain chemistry that has evolved to inform us that one or more of our basic needs is being satisfied. Using drugs is the client's best effort to reduce the pain or frustration in his or her life. The sure pleasure effects of the drug and the total relief of the pain of frustration takes over their minds. Treatment of addicts involves letting them see that settling for normal pleasures in life can satisfy their basic needs better than the pleasures of the drug. Life's pleasures are less intense, but longer lasting. If clients can start enjoying the normal pleasures of life, they can keep the desire for the drug-induced pleasure in check. They can maintain control of their lives instead of relinquishing it to the addiction of the drug. Many clients state that the desire for the drug-induced pleasure never really goes away, but it can be controlled with less and less effort as normal pleasures become a part of their behavioral system and quality world. For example, in Appendix A, Lute said that the joy in seeing his child take its first step was what motivated him to change.

There is an epidemic of loneliness among people in our world. Everywhere, men, women, and children are living as though in plastic bubbles which prevent contact with others. They are cut off from closeness with their brothers and sisters, their own children, partners, co-workers, and neighbors. They have learned to play the role, be efficient, and look good. They ask themselves, *Do I dare let others know how I feel? Will others look down on me? Will others think I am strange?*

All this has made people ripe for the diseases of addiction and codependency. Some of them have romanticized the pain of loneliness and glorified it. They sought some comfort for their pain, but only perpetuated it. Breaking through the barrier to let someone know us can be incredibly difficult, yet, just to say, "I feel lonely" to another person makes us slightly less alone. The greatest benefit of Choice Theory for many addicted people is the newfound ability to deal with loneliness and the genuine relationships they have developed.

Anger alters the mood of the individual by generating adrenalin within the body. Adrenalin gives the person additional energy and a presence of being. Adrenalin can be classified as a mood altering drug and an individual can become addicted to it just like any other drug. This fact sheds some light on the treatment of aggressors.

The only effective treatment, no matter what the method of therapy, is the same with addicts as with other clients:

1. Focus on helping all clients to learn new behaviors to recapture old relationships or gain new ones. The relationships need to be satisfying enough so that the addict no longer needs the drugs.
2. Therapists or loved ones should not try to force or pressure any client to change. To use external control to try to persuade clients to change would be counterproductive because they are very sensitive to external control. Everyone has been trying to tell them what to do during their entire lives and that is why they are sensitive to and want to escape from external control.

External control is the commonplace psychology in society. The client thinks that everyone important to him is *threatening, punishing, criticizing, blaming, complaining, nagging,* and *enabling* him to try to get him to stop using the drug.

The question that needs to be asked of the client is, "Does drinking or using help you get closer to the people that you want and need in your life?" This question places the decision to make a choice on the client. The client will learn to make a choice based on basic needs instead of someone else using external control to pressure the client into not using.

When others around the client use the seven caring habits, the client feels more inclined to make choices based on his relationships and his basic needs.

AA advocates self-responsibility and honesty in the life of the addict. The twelve steps are suggested as a way of life that embraces the tenets of Choice Theory as centered on abstinence of alcohol or the drug of choice. Alcoholics drink to get the feeling that they have escaped the control of others. One of the side effects of drinking alcohol is that the more one drinks, the more one loses control over one's own thoughts, actions, and life. *In a large part, the reason Reality Therapy with Choice Theory works is that it gives alcoholics a respite from external control without alcohol.*

Learning Choice Theory during group sessions and practicing it between group sessions helps clients to realize they can meet their basic needs without the use of drugs or alcohol or the violence that often is associated with them. Glasser states, "What happened in the past that was painful has a great deal to do with what we are today, but revisiting this painful past can contribute little or nothing to what we need to do now: improve an important, present relationship."

Larry's Story

At one meeting, Larry related his uncle was physically threatening Larry's grandmother, with whom the uncle lived. Larry said he heard his uncle yelling and threatening his grandmother in the background when his grandmother called him for help. Larry went to his grandmother's home and, without confronting his uncle, packed some things for her, got her in her wheelchair, and took her to his home.

Larry and his wife were in family counseling in addition to the domestic violence group that Larry attended and he had asked his wife not to discuss the problems with anyone unless it was at the counselor's office. Larry's grandmother was staying in the baby's bedroom where they had a monitor installed. The first night that Larry's grandmother was at his home, his wife went in to the baby's bedroom, and started talking to his grandmother about their problem and the fight they had had. Larry was in the master bedroom and overheard the conversation. He became very angry and wanted to confront his wife. He had the proof and wanted to take out his anger on her. Larry was really ready to let his wife have it. When she came into the bedroom, Larry started to confront her with a great deal of anger in his voice. Larry said that at that point he envisioned the poster on the group meeting room's wall—The Ultimate Question—and stopped his angry confrontation. Every time he tried to say something angry toward his wife, he saw the poster and stopped. Larry said that he got so angry at me for having the poster on the wall and talking about it in group that he quietly cursed me and the poster out for about a half an hour. The next day he calmed down and realized that his wife probably needed to get some of the past off her chest by talking it out with his grandmother. He apologized to his wife for the one outburst and that was the end of the situation. When he reported it to the group, he said, "Boy, was I angry with you for spoiling all of my fun. I was all really ready to get her because I had her dead to rights. Not only could I not yell at my wife for what she had done, but I even had to apologize to her for my angrily confronting her the day before." I just smiled and thought to myself that we must have established a caring relationship with him if he brought to mind the group's concepts in a time of great frustration and anger.

Denial

One of the major contributors to the continuation of aggression in the home is denial by all parties. Two examples are denial that the violence is happening and denial that the violence is as bad as it really is. This is a major issue in the treatment of the aggressor. Facing this denial brings happiness back to the family. Reality Therapy and Choice Theory let the aggressor make a realistic self-evaluation. With this evaluation, aggressors can move beyond denial into a more realistic picture of their total behavior and its effects on others. Many women do not expose the violence they endure to their communities because they think aggression by their mate is *their lot in life*. Most men who are violent in the home excuse it as being their right and deny that it is beyond reasonable arguing. Victims of violence often decide they are trapped in the relationship because they cannot see any way out to live on their own. This is especially true if they do not have a profession or job skills and if they have children. The aggressive person plays on this trapped feeling by convincing the mate that she cannot take care of the family without the help of the aggressor. Denial is at the center of the cycle of violence, and it is what allows the circle to continue. This denial often takes the form of hope, when the spouse hopes that the aggressor will change. The aggressor seldom changes without help (information) from outside sources like counseling.

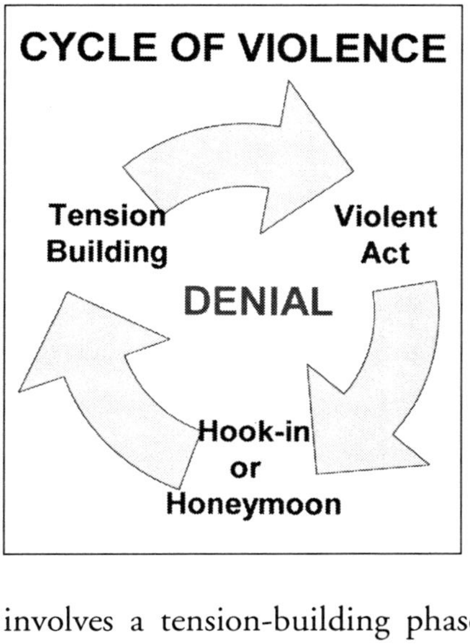
CYCLE OF VIOLENCE
Tension Building
Violent Act
DENIAL
Hook-in or Honeymoon

Family aggression is not limited to physical abuse and threats; it also includes emotional and verbal harassment and any unwanted sexual activity. Many aggressive incidents follow a common pattern called the *cycle of violence*. What happens during the cycle can help explain why some victims feel so guilty and ashamed of their partner's violence toward them. It also explains why they may find it difficult to leave, even when their lives are in danger. The cycle of violence involves a tension-building phase, and then continues with a violent incident followed by a period of loving closeness or reconciliation. Finally, the cycle repeats with another tension-building phase. When a batterer starts to feel he is losing power and control, he tries to get it back in many ways. He uses intimidation, threats, coercion. He might say that he will commit suicide, or report her to welfare if you do not drop the charges, or say he is going to Department of Social Services or immigration. He might not batter the woman, but he will kick other things around, kick the dog, and put a gun or a knife on top of a table or in his pocket. He might call her names or humiliate her in front of others.

The Tension-building Phase

The first phase in the cycle of violence is characterized by tension between the batterer and victim. While stress is a normal factor in all relationships, some people, for a variety of reasons, react to it violently. During the tension-building phase, the woman senses her partner's increasing agitation. She may or may not know what is wrong. Her partner lashes out at her in anger, challenging her, saying she is stupid, incompetent, and unconcerned about his welfare.

During the increasing tension, either the woman becomes angry or she internalizes her anger and suffers depression, anxiety, and a sense of helplessness. The woman often accepts the blame and tries hard not to make any mistakes or say something that may upset her partner. She takes responsibility for making him feel better, setting herself up to feel guilty when he eventually explodes in spite of her best efforts to please him. She may even have physical symptoms related to her emotional distress, such as headaches, upset stomach, insomnia, or fatigue. The woman is not using Choice Theory in dealing with the angering man. If she were, she would not take responsibility for making the man feel better. These problems increase her sense of worthlessness, loss of control, and vulnerability to her partner's criticisms.

The woman may deny her fear and minimize the seriousness of the threat, believing she can control the situation. Even if she acknowledges the danger, she may be reluctant to seek help. She feels ashamed of her failure to please her partner, and she believes that if other people knew about the violence, they would blame her. As the tension increases, so do minor episodes of violence such as pinching, tripping, slapping, or shoving. The batterer knows his behavior is inappropriate and he fears the woman will leave him. That fear of rejection and loss increases his rage at his partner and his need to control her. If the woman returns his anger with anger or defiance, the tension-building phase is shortened and the couple proceeds directly to the violent episode.

During this phase, the couple's children are also affected. They may feel tense, afraid, angry, or confused. They may side with one or the other parent, hide, deny what is happening, or try to distract their parents. Peace may be present during this phase, but happiness is not.

The Violent Episode

The tension-building phase ends in an explosion of violence. The violence may start out as shouting, but it will progress to pushing and shoving and then to hitting. Much of the denial mentioned above comes during the shouting and pushing phases. The incident that sets off the aggressor's violent behavior is often trivial or unknown, leaving the partner feeling desperately confused and helpless. During the episode, the batterer is out of control and often unaware of how much injury he is inflicting. The partner may or may not fight back. The victim often tries to escape the violence; she may call for help. If she cannot escape the beating, she may make herself feel as if it is happening in a dream. She may not be aware of how badly she is being hurt.

Children may be harmed as well. Those who witness the violence may feel frightened or trapped. They may watch helplessly or hide; they may even attempt to stop the fighting or try to help the victim. Children caught in the crossfire of family aggression can become unintended victims of serious injuries when objects are thrown or weapons are used. In addition, youngsters who hear but do not see the violence may suffer emotional trauma.

Following the battering, the victim may be in a state of physical and psychological shock. She may be passive and withdrawn or hysterical and incoherent. She may be unaware of the seriousness of her injuries and resist getting treatment. The batterer discounts the episode and usually underestimates the harm he has inflicted. The batterer may refuse to summon medical help, even if the victim's injuries are life-threatening. Neither peace nor happiness is present during this phase.

The Hook-in or Honeymoon Phase

The hook-in phase is often one of loving reconciliation, also called the *honeymoon* or *remorseful* phase, and begins a few hours to several days after the violent episode. Both the man and the woman have a profound sense of relief that it is over. While the victim may be initially angry with her partner, the aggressor begins an intense campaign to win the victim back. Just as the aggressor's tension and violence were overdone, his apologies, gifts, and gestures of love may also be excessive; he may shower his partner with love and praise that temporarily helps repair the partner's shattered self-esteem. Alternatively, the batterer may threaten to take the children from the victim or divorce the victim if she reports the batterer's actions. The aggressor will try to convince the victim that the courts will not let her have the children because she does not have a place to live and does not have any means to provide a living. It is very difficult for the victim to leave the batterer during this period, since the batterer is meeting the victim's desperate need to see herself as a competent and lovable woman.

In addition, the victim's feelings of power and romantic ideals are nurtured. The victim believes this gentle, loving person is her real mate. If the victim can only find the key, she can control the batterer and prevent further violent episodes. No matter how often the violence has happened before, somehow, this episode seems different; this time, it will never happen again. During the loving reconciliation, a strong bond develops between the couple, isolating them both from reality and from anyone who tries to intervene in their destructive relationship. Friends or family who have supported the victim and urged her to get out of the violent situation may now be seen as enemies trying to separate the loving couple.

Meanwhile, children living in the home during this period may express feelings of embarrassment, humiliation, relief, guilt, or anger. They may try to please their parents or attempt to distract themselves to forget the stress of the battering incident.

The loving reconciliation is a time of intense pleasure and reassurance for the couple that convinces them there is nothing wrong with their relationship. Their isolation discourages them from seeking assistance, and when the violence happens again, the victim may find that she has fewer places to turn for support. Psychologists have found that any behavior followed by a positive reward happens more and more frequently. Thus, the loving reconciliation becomes a kind of reward for the violence. The more often periods of uncomfortable tension end in violent explosions followed by loving closeness, the less likely the couple will be to develop alternatives for handling stress. Moreover, it is this cycle that must be broken in order to end the violence.

Peace is there, but happiness is not present during this phase, either. What is present instead of happiness is the relief that the tension and violence has subsided and the hope that it will not come again—but it does.

The Increasing Spiral of Violence

One aspect of family violence that is particularly troubling is the progressive, spiraling nature of the problem. Once violence has begun, research indicates that it not only continues, but increases over time in both frequency and severity. The three-phase cycle also begins to change. The tension-building phases become shorter and more intense, the acute battering incidents more frequent and severe, and the honeymoon phase is shorter and less intense. After many years of battering, the man may no longer apologize at all. The violence is very much an addiction with the need for more, more often.

For the victim, the psychological consequences of the increasingly severe cycle of violence are feelings and behaviors that form another vicious cycle. She develops behavior patterns in response to the violence that function as traps that keep her from escaping. The escalating violence increases her need, but decreases her ability, to find alternatives to the violent situation.

Most abuse victims fear for their lives and the lives of their children. They may have tried to leave before, only to be found by their partners and abused or punished even worse than before. Such victims often believe that there is no help for them. Understanding the psychological consequences of the violent relationship can help a woman to choose constructive life alternatives. Two stories illustrate how desperate the victim can become.

The first is one that I observed when I was in court on a non-related matter. I observed the victim take the witness stand in a wheelchair. Her right leg was in a full cast from her foot to her thigh. The leg was supported straight out in front of her as she sat. Her right arm and shoulder was also in a cast so that when she swore to tell the truth she had to raise her left hand. Her face looked like she had been badly beaten by someone much larger than she. The eyes were black and blue and the lips were cut and swollen. When asked about the night in question, she said that she had fallen down the stairs and broken her leg and arm. She said that her husband had called 911 and then covered her with a blanket so she would not become chilled and put a pillow under her head to comfort her. She told the court that her husband was very supportive of her and tried to comfort her while they waited for the ambulance to arrive. When the ambulance arrived, there were police officers, too. She said that she had told them what had happened, but they arrested her husband anyway.

The district attorney then called the police officer that had made the report of domestic violence. He testified that, when he got to the home, he found the victim on the floor with a blanket over her and a pillow under her head, just as she had testified. He stated that the victim had told him that her husband had gotten angry, had thrown her against the wall, and beat her up. He testified that she said that he had tossed her around the living room, knocking the furniture over. The officer continued by stating that she told him that her husband had picked her up and slammed her down on the dining room table, breaking it. The district attorney then asked the officer to describe the home as he had found it. The officer stated that the living room and dining room were in disarray with furniture scattered all over the place. He said that there were chairs tipped over and that a lamp was broken on the floor. He said that the dining room table was broken in half where the victim was thrown down on it. Further testimony revealed that there was a dent in the wall where she had been thrown up against the wall. When the officer finished, the district attorney asked him to describe the floor plan of the house. The officer stated that the house was a one story home with no stairs.

This victim was so frightened of her aggressor or of living alone without him that, she completely fabricated the story about falling down the stairs in order to cover up the violence that had been going on in her home for some time. When the district attorney continued with her cross examination, the victim admitted that her husband had been aggressive toward her since they met, but she countered that she loved him and that he could be sweet and loving to her. Children were not mentioned in the portion that I overheard, but if children witnessed any of the violence, they, too, suffer from it.

The second illustration comes from a time when I responded, as a child abuse investigator, to a law enforcement call. A house had burned down and a methamphetamine lab was found in the wreckage. Children living in the home may have been exposed to the deadly chemicals used to manufacture the drugs. When I arrived at the home, I interviewed the children and their mother. The children said that their father had been manufacturing chemicals in the recreation room and that they had been at an aunt's home when the fire happened so they did not know anything about it. The mother said that she had gotten into an argument with father and could see that he was very angry. She went to call 911 when she saw him walking around the living room with a five-gallon can under his arm, spilling something that smelled like fingernail polish on the carpet. (The firefighters stated that the fire was started with acetone.) The mother said to me, "As I dialed 911, I felt heat on the back of my legs and when I turned around, the living room went whoosh." The mother told me that she ran out of the house through the kitchen door because the fire was blocking the front door and hallway. I concluded that if the children had been in their rooms, they would not have been able to escape and might have died as a result of the fire. The police took the father into custody and the mother arranged to stay with a relative. Because of the risk of chemicals and fire to the children, along with the fact that the mother had known about the methamphetamine manufacturing and did not protect the children from the dangers, the children were placed in a foster home for their protection.

When the mother went to court to testify about the events of the fire, she testified that she "might have tipped over a bottle of fingernail polish" (acetone) which caught fire and burnt the house. By saying this, the mother was taking responsibility for the fire and trying to protect her husband from being charged with domestic violence and injury to a firefighter. I asked the district attorney why the mother might have testified as she did. I was told that her husband was giving her over $1,000 a week in cash as her share of the profits from the sale of the methamphetamine. The reason for the denial by mother, in this case, became very clear. She was willing to take responsibility for the fire and continue living with a man who was violent toward her for the money that he paid her. Even with her children taken from her, she was willing to lie in court to protect her husband and the money she was getting from his illegal activities. The children were released to some relatives that were judged to be able to provide a protective home environment until the mother could provide a *safe* home for the children.

When I relate these stories to the group, they began to see just how powerful denial can be in continuing the aggression in the home. This helps them to overcome their own denial and come to grips with the violence that was in their homes. Often the aggression and violence in a client's home is less than that described above, and the client is quick to make that point. The level of violence in the home is less important than the fact that there was any violence, because even a little amount of violence is unacceptable in a loving and caring relationship—one that uses the caring habits and is peaceful and happy. Having the client admit that there was violence in the home is the first step in getting him to face the difficulty in establishing and maintaining a long-term loving relationship with a partner. Making an accurate self-evaluation of your behaviors is one of the major elements in Reality Therapy, as will be shown in the example of Mike's aggression toward Judy in Part II of this book. This evaluation is important in starting on the path of recovery from the use of violence or aggression to deal with frustration, and of physical force as a method for solving your problems.

This second incident is an example of how the community came together to deal with a family situation involving angering. The fire department and police department dealt with the immediate situation in the home and the detective work about the condition of the home; the district attorney prosecuted the father for his illegal activities; Children's Services evaluated the safety of children, arranged for a safe living situation for them, and took responsibility for mother's education regarding her parenting skills; and we, the people—the relatives—took care of the children until the mother could complete her parenting education and provide a safe environment for the children.

CHAPTER 5

Anger Management

Understanding the physiology of anger has important implications in managing anger. First, when anger is chosen, the sympathetic nervous system is activated, which in turn activates certain chemicals—e.g., adrenaline and noradrenalin—that are released from the adrenal glands. These chemicals energize the body to get ready for action, whatever that action might be. Physical symptoms can include rapid heart rate, increased blood pressure, rapid shallow breathing, increased muscle tension, and sweating. Over time, other chemicals will break down the adrenaline in the body and the parasympathetic nervous system will intervene to calm the body down. A person can take certain actions while waiting for the parasympathetic nervous system to intervene. These are called anger management techniques.

In addition to becoming aware of anger, aggressors need to develop strategies to manage it effectively. These strategies can be used to stop the escalation of anger before they lose control and experience negative consequences. An effective set of strategies for controlling anger should include both immediate and preventive strategies. Immediate strategies include taking a time-out, deep-breathing exercises, and thought stopping. Preventive strategies include developing an exercise program and changing irrational beliefs. These strategies are discussed in detail in the group sessions.

Anger management techniques and strategies are taught in groups so that the aggressors can learn how to maintain control of their anger and compulsion to be physically aggressive. These techniques begin to replace the behaviors they learned over their many years of dealing with frustration in their homes of origin and in their neighborhoods and military careers (if they had one) or incarceration (if they served time in a prison).

The clients of both domestic violence groups and parenting groups are shown that there is always going to be frustration caused by the differences between their quality world and their perceived world. They are encouraged to change their behavioral system, perceptions, and total behavior so that their interaction with the real world brings about satisfaction of their basic needs.

One of the anger management tools presented is the anger curve. Clients are shown how it applies to their self-control of anger. The clients can modify their total behavior by learning about their physiology and recognizing the symptoms before they lose control of themselves. The curve illustrates this point.

There is a period when the anger level is in the frustration range and it is building toward rage and a violent act. During this build-up period, the client can sense their feelings and physiology and recognize that they are heading toward the point. The build-up period is indicated by the circle and car. The loss of cognitive control over actions, "point of no return," is indicated by the line near the top of the apex of the curve that represents the violent act.

An important aspect of anger monitoring is to identify the cues that occur in response to the anger-provoking event. These cues serve as warning signs that a person has become angry and that the anger is continuing to escalate. The clues can be broken down into four cue categories: physiological, action, feeling, and thought.

Physiological Cues

Physical cues involve the way our bodies respond when we become angry. For example, our heart rates may increase, we may feel tightness in our chests, we narrow our eyes and wrinkle our foreheads, our faces become taut, or we may feel hot and flushed. These physical cues can also warn us that our anger is escalating out of control or approaching a ten on the anger meter. We can learn to identify these cues when they occur in response to an anger-provoking event.

Can you identify some of the physical cues you have experienced when you have become angry? Some of them were mentioned at the beginning of the chapter.

Action Cues

Action cues involve the behaviors we display when we get angry, which are observed by other people around us. For example, we may clench our fists, pace back and forth, slam a door, speed up in our cars to get alongside of another driver, use curse words, and start to use the deadly habits or raise our voices. These behavioral responses are the second cue of anger. As with physical cues, they are warning signs that we may be approaching the point of no return.

What are some of the action cues that you have experienced just before you have lost control of your temper?

Feeling Cues

Feeling cues involve other feelings that may occur concurrently with our anger. For example, we may become angry when we feel abandoned, afraid, discounted, disrespected, guilty, humiliated, impatient, insecure, jealous, lonely, or rejected. These kinds of feelings are the core or primary feelings that underlie our anger. It is easy to discount some primary feelings because they often make us feel vulnerable. An important component of anger management is to become aware of, and to recognize, the primary feelings that underlie our anger. In the group, we view anger as a secondary emotion to these more primary feelings.

Can you identify some of the primary feelings that you have experienced during an episode of angering?

Thought Cues

Thought cues refer to the thoughts that occur in response to the anger-provoking event. When people become angry, they interpret events in certain ways. For example, we may interpret a friend's comments as criticism, or we may interpret the actions of others as demeaning, humiliating, or controlling. Some people call these thoughts *self-talk*, because they resemble a conversation we are having with ourselves. For people with anger problems, this self-talk is usually very critical and hostile in tone and content. We may think with curse words when we self-talk about other people. This self-talk reflects beliefs about the way we think the world should be: beliefs about people, places, and things.

Closely related to thoughts and self-talk are fantasies and images. We view fantasies and images as other types of cognitive cues that can indicate an escalation of anger. For example, we might fantasize about seeking revenge on a perceived enemy or imagine and visualize our spouse as having an affair. When we have these fantasies and images, our anger can escalate even more rapidly.

Can you think of other examples of cognitive or thought cues?

Once we reach the point of no return, which is different for each person, we have little chance of stopping the progression toward a violent act. Cognitively practicing self awareness of our state of being modifies our behavioral system and makes this awareness a more consistent behavior. This makes it easier for us to deal with the frustration or anger before it reaches the point of no return. This concept is related to the chart through the behavioral system and total behavior.

To break the angering habit and bring peace and happiness into our lives, we must develop an awareness of the events, circumstances, and behaviors of others that trigger our anger before we reach the point of no return. This awareness also involves understanding the negative consequences that result from angering. For example, we may be in line at the supermarket and become impatient because the lines are too long. We could start angering and boisterously demand that the checkout clerk call for more help. As our anger escalates, we may become involved in a heated exchange with the clerk or another customer. The store manager may respond by having a security officer remove us from the store. The negative consequences that result from this event are not getting the groceries that we wanted and the embarrassment and humiliation we suffer from being removed from the store.

The ABCs of Anger

Albert Ellis developed a model that he calls the A-B-C-D or rational-emotive model. In this model, "A" stands for an activating event, what I have been calling the red-flag event. "B" represents the beliefs or perceptions people have about the activating event. It is not the events themselves that produce feelings such as anger, but our interpretations of and beliefs about the events. "C" stands for the feeling or emotional consequences of events. In other words, these are the feelings people experience as a result of their interpretations of and beliefs concerning the event. "D" is the dispute that we have with ourselves over the validity of the beliefs.

According to Ellis and other cognitive behavioral theorists, as people choose angering, they engage in the internal dialogue of self-talk. For example, suppose you were waiting for a bus to arrive. As it approaches, several people push in front of you to board. In this situation, you may choose angering as your total behavior. You may be thinking, "How can people be so inconsiderate! They just push me aside to get on the bus. They obviously do not care about me or other people." Examples of the irrational self-talk that can produce anger escalation are reflected in statements such as, "People should be more considerate of my feelings," "How dare they be so inconsiderate and disrespectful," and "They obviously don't care about anyone but themselves."

Ellis says that people do not have to choose angering when they encounter such an event. The event itself does not get them upset and angry; rather, it is people's interpretations of and beliefs concerning the event that cause them to anger. Beliefs underlying anger often take the form of *should* and *must*. Most people may agree, for example, that respecting others is an admirable quality. Our belief might be, "People should *always* respect others." In reality, however, people often do not respect each other in everyday encounters. You can choose to view the situation more realistically as an unfortunate defect of human beings, or you can choose to let your anger escalate every time you witness, or are the recipient of, another person's disrespect. Unfortunately, the perceived disrespect will keep you angry and push you toward the explosion phase. Ironically, it may even lead you to show disrespect to others, which would violate your own fundamental belief about how people should be treated.

Ellis' approach consists of identifying irrational beliefs and disputing them with more rational or realistic perspectives. A person may choose angering, for example, when he or she starts thinking, "I must always be in control. I must control every situation." It is not possible or appropriate, however, to control every situation. Rather than continue with these beliefs, the person can try to dispute them. He might tell himself, "I have no power over things I cannot control and other people," or, "I have to accept what I cannot change." These are examples of ways to dispute beliefs that he or she may have already encountered in twelve-step programs such as Alcoholics Anonymous or Narcotics Anonymous.

People may have many other irrational beliefs that lead them to choose angering. Consider an example where a friend of yours disagrees with you. You may start to think, "Everyone must like me and give me approval." If you hold such a belief, you are likely to get upset and angry when you face rejection. However, if you dispute this irrational belief by saying, "I can't please everyone; some people are not going to approve of everything I do," you will most likely start to calm down and be able to control your angering more easily.

Another common irrational belief is, "I must be respected and treated fairly by everyone." This also is likely to lead to frustration and anger. Most folks, for example, live in an urban society where they may not always be given the common courtesy they expect. This is unfortunate, but from an anger management perspective, it is better to accept the unfairness and lack of interpersonal connectedness that can result from living in an urban society. Thus, to dispute this belief, it is helpful to think, "I can't expect to be treated fairly by everyone."

Other beliefs that may lead to angering include, "Everyone should follow the rules," or "Life should be fair," or "Good should prevail over evil," or "People should always do the right thing." These beliefs are not always followed by everyone in society, and, usually, there is little you can do to change that. In other words, what thoughts that are more rational and adaptive, and will not lead to anger, can be substituted for such beliefs?

For people with angering and control problems, irrational beliefs such as these can lead to violent acts and to the negative consequences of the real world. It is often better to change their outlook by disputing their beliefs and creating an internal dialogue or self-talk that is more rational and adaptive. It can bring peace and happiness into their lives.

Antecedent

Antecedents come before or trigger, but do not cause, anger. They occur at the beginning of the build-up phase. This is an important distinction to remember. Anyone or anything with which you come into contact on a daily basis can serve as an antecedent for your anger. It is important to recognize and accept that you have no control over the antecedents in your life.

Beliefs

These are the thoughts about the antecedent. The beliefs come from the quality world and are applied to the perceptions that come from the antecedent. Beliefs can be either helpful or unhelpful for you, others, and your important relationships. Each of us can think differently about the same activator. We have total control over our beliefs about a particular activator and can change them when we decide they are no longer satisfying our basic needs.

Beliefs that we often choose to make an aggressive action typically include red-flag words like *should*, *must*, and *ought to*. To this part of our beliefs, these words constitute demands made of, and commands given to, others. They are often inflexible. They are external control words and are one of the deadly habits.

We may conceal our aggression in the form of a question. For example, when we are late for an important meeting and a slower car, driven by an older person, is blocking our path, we might angrily ask ourselves, "Why do they let old people like that drive?" The angering belief in this case would be, "They should not let old people drive."

Consequences

These are the feelings, such as anger or irritation, that you experience, the actions you engage in, and the physiology you create for yourself when you hold certain beliefs about the antecedent. Your actions might include throwing things, cursing, and slamming the wall with your fist. Physical consequences (physiology) might include your muscles getting tense, heart racing, blood pressure increasing, and hands beginning to shake.

Dispute

This is a fancy way of saying that we need to argue against our beliefs. This is the most difficult part of the anger management process because we think that anger helps us control others and it makes us feel powerful. This is an internal self-evaluation of the predicted effectiveness of our total behavior.

Once we are past the incident, we can make some changes in our perceptional system and our behavioral system. Continuing with the ABCD theme, E and F are as follows.

Effective Beliefs

Once we have successfully disputed the old beliefs, usually we need to replace them with effective beliefs that result in happiness. Angering beliefs are commanding and demanding in nature and include words such as should and must. Effective beliefs include words such as wishing, hoping, desiring, preferring, and wanting. These beliefs recognize that we have no control over the antecedent.

New Feelings

Here we re-rate the original total behavior after substituting the more effective beliefs for our angering beliefs. It is this new total behavior that we demonstrate to the real world for evaluation and modification to antecedent.

Barnes Boffey (1997) introduced a way of helping to self-evaluate and create a unifying vision of oneself. He has aggressors ask themselves, "If I have the courage to be the person I wanted to be, how would I handle my present situation?"

Boffey suggests that aggressors should act as if they were that person. He has them keep the following guidelines in mind as they select the new behavior.

- Be realistic. The step you select should be simple and within your grasp; chose something you are sure you can do. We do not want any failures.
- Be unconditional. Resolve to choose this new behavior regardless of how others behave—not only if they do this or that.
- Be committed. Be clear that you will do this—not that you will try or intend to do it. The level of commitment should be, at least, four on a scale from one to five—five being most committed.

Once you have selected your new behavior, state what you will do differently—right away.

Another technique taught in groups that the members are encouraged to practice is the time-out. The time-out is used as a method of gaining control of your physiology before it reaches the point of no return. Time-out is not used as a means of punishment or isolation from others. Several key points to the time-out are stressed as it is used. The first is that the method must be agreed upon by both parties. Time-outs can be used with both children and adults. The agreement is preferably discussed when there is calmness in the relationship and the technique can be broached without putting the mate or children on the defensive. One suggestion is that the client mentions it as something that was discussed in group and that he or she would like to try it so that the family can come to a negotiated difference instead of having another argument. If the mate or child agrees to try the time-out method, they proceed as follows. Either person can ask for a time-out period not to exceed sixty minutes so that they can regain control of themselves. With children, the time period should equal their age, up to ten minutes. This way the client is taking responsibility for his or her total behavior and not placing any responsibility on the mate or child. A kitchen timer is one way to keep track of the time.

If either party recognizes the early warning signs of anger described above, he or she can call a personal time-out by telling the other person that he or she is angering and will need to separate for a period of time. Once the time-out is called, both people stop the discussion or argument and retreat to another activity or quiet place that will take their minds off the subject. This allows them to regain their composure and return to the subject with a calmer and more objective manner. At the end of the agreed-upon time, they come back together to discuss the subject. If either party starts to increase the level of anger, he or she should ask for another time-out period. When both parties are calm enough to negotiate their differences, the discussion must continue. Remember that taking a time-out also requires you to take a *time-in*. Taking a time-out is one way to regain control of yourself, rather than saying or doing something that hurts you or others as you would have done in the past. It is using the ultimate question and caring behaviors. Time-out is not a way to get out of settling the issue and should not be used to put the problem away until it can be brought up to win another argument. Once the problem has been solved, the relationship will return to a more peaceful and satisfactory state.

Managing anger is a matter of stress reduction because stress and anxiety are major influencing factors of anger and its violent expression. Reducing stress and anxiety reduces the energy level and the likelihood of violence in the expression of anger. Some of the ways to reduce the stress that builds up from daily activities are taking a deep breath, exercising, eating well, gardening, getting a massage, meditating, getting enough sleep, trying guided imagery, getting a pet, keeping a journal, holding family meetings, talking privately with your spouse, trying progressive relaxation, planning getaways, being assertive, taking a day off, delegating, enlisting a sympathetic ear, setting priorities, or making a list.

People use assertiveness to deal with the frustration of powerlessness. The success is not in the gaining what they want, but in asking for what they want. When assertive behavior is used, it does not demean others, but it allows one to express the frustration that is felt over a situation and requests that others assist in changing the situation to lessen the feelings of powerlessness.

The acting out of anger is the root of family violence. Understanding the causes of hostility is relevant to all who work in the field of family violence and parenting and their related studies.

Many techniques are discussed in the groups as part of the giving of information on the ways to manage the anger in the family and the discipline of the children. These techniques are discussed in many anger management and parenting texts and lectures. One of the goals of anger management is to realize that it is not the person, the behavior, or even the event that leads a person to choose angering. Rather, it is how the person chooses to think (their beliefs) regarding the other person, behavior, or event which triggers their anger. Anger has many negative natural real-world consequences. Anger often leads to verbal and physical aggression and decreased problem solving. Clients are encouraged to examine their anger-causing beliefs and replace them with caring habits, with assertiveness, and with increased problem-solving total behavior.

One of the most important ideas to keep in mind when dealing with people who are hard to get along with is not to be controlled by them. These people often resort to control maneuvers in order to get their needs met. When a client finds himself fighting all of the time, a lot of mutual controlling is going on between him and the other person. It is up to each person in the relationship to stop his or her input to the fight or controlling behavior. The client can always choose not to fight. This is a very important first step in changing his or her total behavior with others.

Conflict Resolution

One method of acting assertively is to use the Conflict Resolution Model, which involves five steps that can easily be memorized.

1. The first step involves *identifying the problem* that is causing the conflict. Consider the problem of your friend being late when you pick him up to go to a meeting of a favorite organization. It is important to be specific when identifying the problem. In this example, the problem causing the conflict is that your friend is late.

2. The second step involves *identifying the feelings* associated with the conflict. In this example, you may feel annoyance, frustration, or taken for granted.

3. The third step involves *identifying the specific impact* of the problem that is causing the conflict. In this example, the impact or outcome is that you are late for the meeting.

4. The fourth step involves *deciding whether to resolve the conflict or let it go*. This may best be phrased by the questions, "Is the conflict important enough to bring up? If I do not try to resolve this issue, will it lead to feelings of anger and resentment?" If you decide that the conflict is important enough, then the fifth step is necessary.

5. The fifth step is to *address and resolve the conflict*. This involves checking out the schedule of the other person. The schedule is important because you might bring up the conflict when the other person does not have the time to address it or when he or she may be preoccupied with another issue. Once you have agreed on a time with the person, you can describe the conflict, your feelings, and the impact of the conflict and ask for a resolution.

For example, the interaction may sound like this:

Jim: Hey, Tom, sorry I'm late.

Tom: Hi, Jim. Can I talk to you about that?

Jim: Sure. Do you have a problem with it?

Tom: Jim, I've noticed you've been late for the last few days when I've come to pick you up. Today, I realized that I was starting to feel frustrated and a bit taken for granted. When you are late, we are both late for the meeting, which makes me uncomfortable. I like to be on time. I'm wondering if you can make an effort to be on time in the future.

Jim: Tom, I didn't realize how bothered you were about that. I apologize for being late, and I will be on time in the future. I'm glad you brought this problem up to me.

The Conflict Resolution Model is useful even when conflicts are not resolved. Many times, we feel better about trying to resolve a conflict in an assertive manner rather than acting passively or aggressively. Specifically, we may feel that we have done all that we could do to resolve the conflict. In this example, if Tom decided not to give Jim a ride in the future, or if Tom decided to end his friendship with Jim, he could do so knowing that he first tried to resolve the conflict in an assertive manner.

The apology that Jim gave Tom included the three main features of a true apology. They are saying that you are sorry, admitting that it was your fault, and determining how to make the situation right.

Negotiating Differences or Fighting Fair

One of the caring habits is negotiating differences. Other authors have called this *fighting fair* but Choice Theory uses the term negotiating differences for this concept. I tell the groups that *fighting* with their partner is illegal, but fighting fair is legal and recommended. How we argue, especially how we end an argument, can determine the long-term success or failure of our relationship. If we negotiate our differences by the rules of the caring habits, an equitable settlement can be reached. A primary requirement for any fight is to maintain control of our total behavior and not that of our mate's or child's. We do not have the license to be childish, abusive, or immature. If we have legitimate feelings, we are entitled to give a reasonable voice to those feelings in a constructive way. (That includes not being self-righteous or taking yourself too seriously.) Remember that the solution to the problem is more important than winning the fight. The basic negotiation outline should be as follows: state the issue, suggest alternatives, and reach a solution. Do not avoid a negotiation or a question in a negotiation. State the issue as a request, not a demand or a speech. Remember that you are not a mind reader or a therapist. Let your partner state his or her views and listen to what the partner says instead of thinking about what you will say next.

Here are eight specific rules for fighting fair that I have modified to include the axioms of Choice Theory.

Do not argue in front of the children.

Children learn how to behave from watching their parents and others. Actions speak louder than words. Full communication consists of three elements—the words, the tone of voice, and the body language. The words make up about 7 percent of total communication, the tone of voice equals about 25 percent, and the remaining 68 percent is attributed to the body language. All we can do is give others information, and we want that information to be positive instead of negative. The information we convey in the written word is about one-fifth of the information that we give over the phone and about one-fourteenth of what we give when talking in person. Even if our children do not hear the fighting, what they see has a great effect on their feeling of stability in the home. Even if they do not see the fight, they see the anger before and after the fight and they feel unsafe in the family. Fighting in front of the children is nothing short of child abuse. It can and will scar them emotionally. The caring habit of negotiating differences is a positive means to settle differing views on a subject. Therefore, doing this in front of children can be a positive learning experience for the children.

Keep to the issue at hand.

The pain that happened in the past has a great deal to do with who we are today. However, revisiting the past pain can contribute little or nothing to what we need to do now: improve an important, present relationship. (This is the tenth axiom of Choice Theory.) Do not bring up old grudges or sore points when they do not belong in a particular argument. Lay boundaries down around the subject matter so that a fight does not deteriorate into a free-for-all.

Maintain reality.

Even though reality is filtered through your perceptions, try to keep the discussion about the facts. Deal with what really is at issue, not with a symptom of the problem. Be honest about what is bothering you, or you will come away from the exchange even more frustrated because you have not negotiated your differences.

Use the caring habits.

Stay focused on the issue instead of deteriorating into an attack on your partner personally. Do not let the fight degenerate into name-calling.

Remain task-oriented.

Work toward a solution and know what you want going into the disagreement. If you do not have a goal in mind, you will not know when you have achieved it.

Allow your partner to retreat with dignity.

Remember that this is a negotiated solution to the problem and not a win-lose battle. The manner in which the argument ends is crucial. Recognize when an olive branch is being extended to you (perhaps in the form of an apology or a joke), and give your partner a face-saving way out of the disagreement. Acceptance of your partner's point of view may be the solution to the fight.

Be proportional in your intensity.

Most of the arguments that you have with people are not the *hill to die on* level of disagreement. Not every single thing you disagree about is an earth-shattering event or issue. You do not have to get mad every time you think you have a right to be. Getting mad is one of the deadly habits and pushes the other person away from you and a solution to your problem. This is contrary to the desire to settle the disagreement.

There's a time limit.

Arguments should be temporary, so do not let them get out of hand. Do not allow the ugliness of an argument to stretch on indefinitely. The longer you fight, the more likely you are to become angry and lose control of yourself. If you have to stop fighting and take a time-out, do so, then come back, and work on a mutual solution together after the time-out has expired. It usually takes no more than two or three sentences to make your point and anything after that is just repeating yourself with the same or different words.

The keys to living with difficult people, as stated by Dr. Primason (2004) are as follows:

- Stay connected without criticizing or fighting;
- Do not be controlled by their behavior—set your limits and walk away from the fight;

- Get some support by finding a friend or partner with whom you can debrief—tell them how hard you are working.

This book does not give an exhaustive treatment of anger management techniques. It is intended to provide the underlying philosophy that will make those techniques useful and successful so that peace and happiness can be restored in the home. There are many anger management books and articles. See them for a more complete discussion on anger management techniques.

Levels of Commitment

The clients' level of commitment indicates the chance of success that the aggressor may have in actually changing their behavioral system. How hard is the client willing to work at solving his or her problem and gaining a better sense of self-control? This is the real question that relates to how successful the aggressor will be and if there will be any recidivism or a change in the aggressor's method of domination over the others in his family. Wubbolding (2000) identified five levels of commitment related to the intensity of motivation. They include the following:

1. "I do not want to be here. The judge sent me and you can't change me. I'm not the problem; she is the one causing all of the trouble."
2. "I want the outcome, but do not want to make the effort. I want people to like me, but I don't want to work for it. I'd like to have a good relationship, but I don't want to change."
3. "I'll try," or "I might," or "I could," or "Maybe," or "Probably, it sounds like a good idea."
4. "I will do my best, but I may fail if she doesn't change, too!"
5. "I will do whatever it takes. Nothing can stop me."

Level One represents no commitment at all and indicates that the external control from the judge has only resulted in resentment on the aggressor's part. It is like saying, "I'll sit here for the fifty-two weeks, but you cannot change me." I tell this level of client that all the group can do is to give him information; what he does with it is his choice. This gives him permission to be stubborn and yet still be receptive to the information that is being presented by me and the other members of the group. These clients are rebelling to the external control of the system that ordered them to attend the group. I immediately give them a choice as to their behavior and let them know that I am not going to force anything upon them. This illustrates to them that it is their choice to learn Choice Theory and practice it in their lives. They will find out later on that they can be happier using the caring habits instead of the deadly habits, but that takes time. Most parents come to the group with a higher level of commitment than Level One because they want to either get their children back or get children's services out of their lives.

Level Two represents a reluctant client. The client does not want to take any action and just wishes that they would become less angry and aggressive and that the family would leave them alone until it happens. The client who came in as a Level One moves to a Level Two after a few weeks when they learn that others have accepted Choice Theory and that I am not forcing it upon them. They begin to accept that I really mean that they can take it or leave it. The choice is theirs. The client would like to have what the other clients are talking about in their relationships and families, but to admit it would mean that they had to admit that they were wrong in the first place. This is extremely hard for some clients to do in public. I do not ask for them to admit that they were wrong. Right and wrong are not a part of Choice Theory; making choices that better satisfy their needs is the major objective and that will bring happiness into their lives.

Level Three indicates that the client may be willing to take action and make a change. This level allows for excuses for failure and reoccurrence of the aggression and poor parenting skills. Commitment at this level is not very satisfying to the victim of the aggression or abuse or the children. The aggressor parent may still require monitoring in visitation circumstances. The client at this level talks about successes in group and supports the Choice Theory concepts to the other group members. The client is willing to bring difficult situations that arise in their relationships to group for discussion, but sometimes argues against the use of Choice Theory concepts. They are fence-sitters as to the determination of making the changes necessary to become a caring person. They are challenging me to prove to them that Choice Theory will be better for them than their old way of external control.

Level Four indicates a higher level of commitment and gives hope to the family and facilitator although there can still be failure and reoccurrence of the aggression and poor parenting skills. This level does not commit the client to 100 percent success, but does restore the hope for a peaceful family and happiness in the future. A client at this level can be reported to the court as accepting and practicing the concepts of non-violent behavior or positive parenting. The judges are happy to receive these reports from the facilitator. The client will now argue in favor of Choice Theory ideas and give examples of how he has utilized them in his relationships. The client still allows for mistakes and reverts back to external control methods on occasion, but is willing to look at those mistakes as learning lessons. Some times these learning lessons do involve the law enforcement and a return to court, but that is part of learning that the real world will always react to any and all of our total behaviors.

Peter's Story

Peter had completed the group as ordered by the court and had accepted the concepts of Choice Theory to a level of at least four and maybe even five. I tell all of the graduating clients that if they feel the need to return to the group to discuss any building anger, they can visit, free of cost, any time they wish. Peter knew this, but kept putting off returning to the class because he thought he would do it if things got a little worse. He was partway up the slope of his anger curve but he did not realize how far he was toward the point of no return. One day he was taking his eight year old son to an appointment when he tried to park his truck. As he pulled into a parking slot and they got out of the truck, he observed two men and a woman arguing over a parking slot. The woman was using curse words and Peter approached and asked her not to use such language in front of his son. The woman immediately took to fighting with Peter and hit him several times in the face before he could react and defend himself. The woman continued the attack and Peter retreated to the bed of his truck and picked up a baseball bat. Peter states that he did not swing the bat at the woman, but the woman and the other two men said that he did. The police came and Peter went to jail. The judge observed Peter's record for domestic violence and the case was set for trial. Peter's lawyer suggested that Peter return to groups to indicate to the judge that he was willing to continue work on his angry responses to such situations. Peter returned to group, promptly admitted his actions, and told the story of what had happened. He realized, albeit too late, that he should have returned to the groups when his anger was building instead of waiting for it to boil over so that the real world had to step in to take control of his behavior. Peter was before, and certainly is now, a strong advocate of Choice Theory and the caring habits for use in his life.

Level Five is the highest level of commitment. This is a real commitment that can be transmitted with confidence to the court and family. Such an aggressor follows through on plans without making excuses for any physical aggression. Until Choice Theory is integrated into his behavioral system and has been practiced under varying circumstances, it will not become routine in the former aggressor's life. However, the client is determined to follow through with the changes needed so that he can live by the caring habits. If a client reaches this level, then he is able to keep the concepts of Choice Theory and the caring habits in the front of his mind and base his actions on satisfying his basic needs, bringing him happiness without denying anyone else the same chance of being happy.

Many clients come into the group with a low level, typically Level One or Two, and as they progress through the fifty-two weeks of the group or the parenting sessions, they move through the levels. Not all of the clients move to Level Five—that would be too much to expect or even hope for. The ones that do not move past Level Two are the ones that have a good chance of repeating their aggression toward their mates and/ or family. This chance of repetition is reported back to the courts when the client has completed the mandated number of sessions. Levels Three and Four show progress, but still leave room for improvement. These clients continue to present a certain amount of risk of family aggression. Those who reach Level Five show a real commitment to live a life without aggression, moving beyond the anger and hurt of the past. Many times, if the former aggressor reaches Level Five while remaining in the previously abusive relationship, the partner and children must change as well. The previous victims see the change in the abuser and decide that they like this new way of behaving so they adopt the concepts of Choice Theory for themselves. When this occurs, the entire family benefits from learning from the aggressor. It is a real pleasure to watch clients move between the levels of commitment and know they are going to be passing this caring way of thinking on to their families and new friends. However, it should be said that a client who has reached a high level of commitment might slip back and choose not to make the effort required to maintain that high level of commitment.

While the Golden Rule states that you should treat others as you would treat yourself, the Choice Theory version differs slightly by bringing the other person's desires into focus: *Treat others as they would want you to treat them.* The difference is based on the fact that we often treat ourselves very poorly and with little respect, as the following story illustrates. The reason for treating others as they would want to be treated instead of how you treat yourself becomes evident.

John's Story

One day in group, John said that he was feeling depressed. His total behavior was that of depressing. He admitted that he was sad, lethargic, judged himself to by worthless, and was inactive. He was having trouble dealing with his family life and the relationship with his ex-wife. He was separated from his children and was having difficulty with his co-workers. We had talked about using the caring habits with others and John said that he was not satisfied with these relationships even though he was trying to use the caring habits instead of the deadly habits. It just didn't seem to be working.

The next week, John came to group and reported that he was doing much better and was feeling good about himself and his life. I asked what had happened during the week to change his total behavior. John explained that he had done some thinking about the caring habits and that he realized that he had to use them with himself before he could use them with anyone else. He said, "I have to care about myself and act as though I do by using the caring habits with myself and not pushing myself away from myself before I can use the caring habits with anyone else." My mouth dropped open and I was speechless at the insight that he had discovered. John had made a major step forward in changing his behavioral system and total behavior choices.

He said that he had to be supportive of himself and his way of life. He stated that he needed to encourage himself to continue to use the caring habits on not only himself, but on others, too. He said that he had to listen to his body and what it was telling him about his happiness and health. He also said that he needed to accept himself where he was at this time, realizing that he was on the correct path to choosing happiness for himself. He stated that he needed to trust what his inner voices were telling him about the improvement he was making and that he could continue with the program. He said that he had to start respecting himself for what he was doing and who he was and that he needed to negotiate the differences in what the old deadly habits behavior would have him do and what the new caring habits behavior requires. He said that he has to negotiate with himself when there are multiple choices that he has to consider a total behavior. Part of this negotiation is to assess what the real world will do in reaction to his total behavior.

His commitment toward making the changes necessary to bring about a happier life had moved to a level that would lead him to success in his goal of obtaining happiness in his life.

CHAPTER 6

Helping Children Become Adults—Parenting

Child rearing is a process that has many great rewards, but it is frustrating at the same time. This chapter addresses some of the parenting concepts that use Choice Theory as their basis. This chapter is included as an introduction to these concepts and to illustrate how to deal with some of the typical children's actions over which parents choose to anger. This book does not present many of the parenting techniques in any additional detail. Instead, you are referred to the many available parenting books and articles. The subsections of this chapter introduce discipline, alternatives to physical or emotional punishment, using the ultimate question with your children, and helping the child to be successful in school. Finally, this chapter concludes with the recognition of child abuse as a result of the angering in the family.

Children bring much joy, happiness, and pleasure into the home if they are parented with love and caring. Parenting can be the most rewarding experience of your life. It can also be the most challenging. Would not it be nice if children came with instructions? Who can you turn to when you have questions? Who can provide the tools you need to be the best parent for your children? Family and friends can help in many situations, and additional resources can provide specific information, education, or the support you need, when you need it. It only takes a few minutes to learn more about the resources available to you and your family. These include

- Parent education programs
- Family support centers

- Well-baby programs
- Child-care programs
- Respite care
- Parent mentor programs
- Parenting classes

Every parent can use support. No matter how great or small the need, there are resources in your community that can give you guidance. Take a minute now and learn about the resources in your community.

Choice Parenting (Primason, 2004) is an excellent book on using Choice Theory with children and is recommended reading for a more through development of the subject of parenting.

Dr. Primason states:

> Parents who use choice psychology are by no means hands-off parents. They love their children and recognize their responsibility to assist in their children's development. Like a caring and careful gardener, choice parents select materials and make important choices in their own behavior. They create the proper conditions for successful growth, but go easy on control. Choice parents are unquestionably involved with their children, offering guidance and listening with interest to the children's view on whatever the latest social or practical challenges may be. The choice parent is in no way an indulgent parent. She recognizes that she must limit her own assistance and allow her children to develop their own plans and solutions.

Raising children to become adults is a multi-year full-time job. It involves discipline, caring, support outside the home, and protection within the home. Discipline is helping children develop self-control; it is not providing the external control for them. It is setting limits and discussing undesirable behavior. Discipline also is encouraging children, guiding them, helping them feel good about themselves, and teaching them how to think for themselves. Spanking is not a good form of discipline. Discipline should help children learn how to control their own behavior. Spanking is used to control children's actions—it is external control. In some countries, spanking is against the law. It does not teach children self-control, as good discipline should. Children do need to know that the adult is in charge, but spanking can teach children to be afraid of the adult in charge. Good discipline teaches children to respect the adult in charge. Respect goes both ways—treat children with respect and let them have control over their own behavior, and they will respect you and listen to you. Children do as you do, not as you say. If you want your children to obey the natural rules of society, solve their own problems, and control their anger, you must set good examples for them to follow. Stay calm and try to do what is appropriate with both you and your child. Sometimes your children can help you decide what is appropriate to do when a rule is broken. Do something that makes sense and will help them learn not to make the same mistake again. For example, if they write on the wall, have them help clean it up. When my son used liquid shoe polish in a squirt gun to write on the wall of his bedroom, he explained that he could not see the water when he wrote on the wall, so he thought that shoe polish would help him to read what he had written. Yes, his mother and I were upset, but it was all we could do to keep from laughing at his explanation of why he had done it. It made perfectly good sense to a little boy of three years old. We got together and helped him wash it off and then re-paint his room to cover it up. He learned the error in his ways, but not by our punishing him or yelling at him. He learned it be having to help clean up the mess. He also learned how to clean and paint walls, which were much more valuable lessons than what he would have learned from being punished or spanked.

Parents who use external control believe it is the parent's job to make sure the child makes good choices. The Choice Theory parent believes that it is the parent's job to help the child learn to make good choices on his or her own. The parent is trying to help the child learn to evaluate his or her own total behavior and make more successful, satisfying choices. Rebellion in adolescents often results from insufficient respect by the parent for the child's heightened need for freedom.

The tell-tale signs of family aggression can be seen when some toddlers play house. They play mommy and daddy and they hit each other. Kids model what they see, but that model can change by giving children—as young as possible—a vision of what life should be. The parent has to change an attitude. They have to educate the child on what is the healthy way to behave and how to control their impulses. While the place to teach children how to control those angry impulses can range from the pre-school classroom to the prison cell, authorities say extra effort must be taken to reach out to youngsters before they begin to follow the violent footsteps of their parents. It is much easier to teach a child to resolve his or her frustration and anger without hurting others, than to correct aggressive behavior after he or she has learned to use it as a means of external control.

There is no way to stop it this year or next year. The only way to reduce aggressive behavior in future years is by recognizing the problem and educating the children. With study after study showing that children reared in violence are more likely to become violent adults, experts in law enforcement, education, and social services insist changing behavior today will pay off tomorrow. Teaching children that everyone should be treated with respect and that violence is never acceptable is an important step. One way we can stop the cycle is by teaching children in school that they do not need to use violence. Teaching healthy communication skills is a long range way to help. Educating boys about women, that women are equal to men, and that boys cannot use violence to get what they want is important. Those in the criminal justice, social service, and education fields say thoughtful and innovative approaches must be taken to address the problem before it worsens.

Dr. Glasser (1984) suggests that there are three ways we can relate to our children. We can do things *to* them, we can do things *for* them, and we can do things *with* them. The first two are of little value. Doing things with your children will bring forth a deeper relationship between you and them and will lead to them doing things in order to keep the relationship healthy and happy. He also suggests that parenting with Choice Theory is really preventive care. If it is used early on in life, the kind of discipline problems that require external control are seldom needed.

In Resa Steindel Brown's book, *The Call to Brilliance* (2006), she quotes her husband, Dennis, as writing:

> We should share in our children's delight at every opportunity. First, it is fun. It is terrific for us and we shouldn't miss it. Inexpensive thrills are hard to find. Second, the children will find their delight reinforced, and they will tend to internalize the capacity to produce it. They will tend to make more of it as the years go by. The ability to produce joy is a skill that is invaluable in later life. People who can find and make their own delight will probably be happier and more socially successful than those who cannot.

I think that this summarizes not only the duty and the joy in raising children, but the rewards of sharing your life with your children. It emphasizes that being a part of your children's lives and sharing in their maturing will provide joy and happiness for all of you for many years to come.

Doing *with* a child is taking responsibility for what you want, respecting the child and what they want, and supporting them to take responsibility for what they want. Responsibility is learning to choose effective behaviors to get what you want and be the person you want to be, while assisting your child to learn to choose effective behaviors to get what they want and become the type of person they want to be. This is effective parenting.

The prime consideration should be the relationship between you and your child. To preserve or improve that relationship, what you might think is best might have to be set aside if it will cause irreversible harm to your child. Learning to respect what the other wants even though you may not agree will accomplish much more with your teen than having each disagreement escalate into a power struggle—win or lose, you always lose. *The secret of a successful relationship between any two individuals when the power is not equal—parent/child or boss/employee—is for the person with the most power to do as much as he can to show respect for the weaker person's position.* The use of external control with your child is probably the most deadly of habits in such a relationship. The use of the seven deadly habits will kill a relationship, whereas the use of the seven caring or connecting habits will nurture it. The paradox is that the more direct control the parent is willing to give up, the more indirect control the parent gains through the stronger and happier relationship with the child.

Punishment and the use of criticism, correction, and coercion are the most frequent ways in which we do things *to* our children. Parents think this provides guidance for their children. Parents are satisfying their power need to be effective and responsible. The children feel oppressed, controlled, and inhibited. To gain an equal footing, they fight back with oppositional behavior, or shut down and often choose to be depressed. Whichever they do, the method is not very effective. Punishment accomplishes a few things for the parent. It may let the parent feel in greater control of the situation, but it will teach the child to be more careful about being caught. The child will be less inclined to create a new solution, will feel less connected with you, and will be less interested in following the parent's suggestions. If this is what you want for your child, then continue angering with him or her and teach him or her what punishment is all about.

Parents who tend to be punitive and authoritarian often try to catch their children in a lie to prove a point. If for example, you find a note in your child's room that refers to a friend's smoking. A trap-setter says, "Do you or your friends smoke? No? What about this note?" As a result, you have a defensive child who learns to lie, conceal, and mistrust parents. A better and more straightforward, trusting inquiry would be, "I found this note in your room that concerns me. Can we talk about it?" Not everything children write is true.

Parents who were raised in dysfunctional families often make the mistake of implying their children are responsible for the circumstances of the parent's life. For example: "Why do you always upset your father? I devoted my life to you and now … If you loved me, you'd do this." The child comes to feel responsible for the problems of the world.

A more effective way of dealing with the situation is to examine your own codependent relationships with your parents, spouse, and others, with a therapist or support group or counselor so that you can improve your current important relationships.

The Problem with Choosing Punishment over Discipline

Some parents make the connection that it was their punishment of the child that made him or her stop the objectionable behavior. They believe that their external control of the child worked. When parents make this connection, it reinforces their tendency to use punishment because punishment seems to have worked. What really happened is that the punishment did not make the child do anything. Rather, the child decided at some point that he or she no longer wished to experience further punishment and chose to cease the behavior you found objectionable. The children remember the punishment and not the lesson that you wanted them to learn.

Many times when working with parents who have punished their children in an abusive manner, I ask the children when the last time their parent spanked, hit, or did some other form of physical punishment was. The children can tell me the exact time of their last punishment, but when I ask them what they had done, they cannot remember. They could only remember the punishment. When parents hear this, they begin to understand that the punishment did not teach their children any lessons, but it did teach them that physical punishment was the thing that parents do to control their children.

Punishment, and the anger that produces it, is based on the myth that you can control others—including your children. You have no control over the antecedents in your life. You can only provide your children with information, and then it is the child that makes the choice as what to do with that information. The only things you can control are your own thoughts and actions concerning your total behavior. Since punishment is based on the myth that we can control others, it fails to recognize that others, including children, are free to make choices concerning whether or not to continue certain behaviors. The decision to either continue or discontinue certain behaviors resides exclusively with the child. In other words, you cannot make a child do anything! The sooner that a parent accepts this fact, the happier will be the relationship between the parent and the child.

Children become resistant to excessive punishment. When this happens, the parent's need to control the child is so great that each time the child resists those efforts, the parent chooses angering and external control and increases the punishment. Eventually these children, who have been punished most of their lives, no longer respond to any type of punishment. At this point, often in the teens, both children and parents are locked in an angering power struggle. The parent must stop his or her choices of punishment to stop this struggle because the child has not been taught how to deal with difficulties on his own and, therefore, cannot stop the struggle. Parents can do this by challenging their anger-producing beliefs and by reminding themselves that they cannot control their children. They can start by using the seven caring habits instead of the seven deadly habits.

In most cases, the use of physical force to get the child to do what you want is counterproductive to obtaining the desired end result.

Example: Pushing or dragging a frightened child into the doctor's office.

The parent is asserting a need for external control rather than responding to the child's feelings, wants, and needs.

Result: The child resists.

A better total behavior is to help the child express his or her feelings, wants, and needs. "Is there something scary in the doctor's office?" Give the child a choice: "Do you want me to hold your hand, or do you want to go in by yourself?" This gives the child a sense of control over the situation, but leaves no question that the child is going into the office.

The final problem with punishment stems from the fact that children often decide not to engage in certain behaviors for which they have been punished in the past, but only as long as the threat of punishment is immediately present. Once the threat of immediate punishment is lifted, children often resume their objectionable behavior. This explains why when children reach their teens, and the freedom that goes with it, they start to act out when they are away from home. They often choose drugs, alcohol, or sex as ways to make a statement about their freedom from punishment. The resulting natural consequences of their choices often result in additional complications with which the parents have to deal.

So what is a parent to do?

The purpose of discipline—from disciple, a student or follower—is to teach the child to have self-discipline. This is never accomplished by physical force. Parents who hit or physically punish their children instill hostility and resentment rather than respect. Usually the behavior is not prevented from recurring, and great damage is done to the parent-child relationship.

Physical punishment tends to repeat in families. If you frequently choose to routinely hit children as a method of discipline, examine your own childhood. Parents who regularly strike their children in frustration or anger usually lack alternative skills, and often have unrealistic expectations of their children at different ages.

One recommendation is to get developmental information on normal child or teen behaviors, and improve parenting skills through many books, magazines, videotapes, support groups, workshops, and other widely available resources.

It is then helpful for parents to reflect on and discuss their expectations for their children. What are the most important two or three values they want to teach their children? What are the two or three behaviors they would like to help their child develop? For teenagers, are there a few non-negotiable actions, such as a consistent message to avoid drinking and driving.

Parents need to first discipline themselves by effectively managing their angering. Then they need to provide information for their children by letting their children experience the natural consequences of their choices. Of course, lasting physical or psychological harm to a child is out of the question as a natural consequence.

Natural consequences are those consequences that flow naturally from the choices we make. For example, if your child does not set his alarm the night before an important test, the natural consequence of that choice would be missing the test and possibly flunking the test. Natural consequences are life's greatest teachers. Parental support and caring is also a part of the natural consequences so that the child knows that the parent is providing unconditional love for the child when the child makes its own choices.

The task of a parent is to guide your children by establishing a range of acceptable choices for any given situation, and then allow them to choose from within that range. The range of choices becomes greater the older the child gets, assuming that he or she has demonstrated good decision making in the past. When your children make wise choices, they get favorable results. When they make poor choices, they experience unfavorable outcomes. By interacting with them in this manner, you avoid the need to punish them and instead, teach them self-discipline; i.e., how to make good choices and behave appropriately when no one is around to threaten punishment. The strength of the relationship between you and your child is the restraining force that the child uses to make better choices.

Punishment is designed to decrease certain behaviors. Rewards are designed to increase certain behaviors. As a parent, it is important to realize that rewarding desired behavior is always more powerful than punishing undesirable behavior. Rather than looking for bad behaviors to punish, start spending more time looking for good behaviors to reward. However, rewarding to control your child is one of the seven deadly habits because the child will only do the desired behavior to get the reward and not because of a good relationship between the two of you. Rewards for your children should not be associated with a particular action every time that action is performed, but rather should be given on occasion when something special has been accomplished or achieved—almost on a random basis if the child is consistently a high achiever.

We love our children and do not want to see them struggle, so we do things for them. The story of the man who was walking in the forest and saw a butterfly struggling to get out of its cocoon illustrates this point. The man went over to the butterfly and very carefully took out his knife and slit open the side of the cocoon so that the butterfly could get out more easily. The beautiful butterfly flew away for about ten yards, then fell to the ground, and died of exhaustion. You see, the butterfly needed to build up his strength and stamina by struggling to get out of the cocoon. When the man made it easier for the butterfly to fly away without developing fully, the butterfly could not live in the world on his own. When we do things for our children instead of letting them learn how to do things for themselves, we deprive them of the strengths they need to survive in the real world when we are not there. One change we can make as parents is to change from doing *to* and doing *for*, to doing *with* our children.

Children are much like my cats, Oscar and Cali. They will come to you when they have a need to be fulfilled. They want love and belonging from you, but they will run from you when they want to be independent. When you give them the love and belonging that they want, they are fulfilled and can go away happy and content. It you do not give them the love and belonging they crave when they want it, they will pester you by getting between you and the newspaper or jumping up onto your lap and sharpening their claws on your legs. They will do this until you give in to them. It is this pestering that most parents choose to become upset and anger over. Most children would rather have negative attention than no attention at all. All attention feeds the love and belonging need. The reason they act out is because you pay attention to them when they are acting out and not when they are behaving. Ordering them around during these times of the child's showing of a love and belonging need destroys the relationship between parent and child—a destruction that is hard to overcome in later years.

One of the other sides of love and belonging is solitude and it is another vital necessity that seems to be in short supply in modern society. Many of us spend so much of our lives in the company of others or engaged in various forms of activity and entertainment that we fear spending time alone. Yet through solitude we can get to know our deeper selves, get in touch with the roots of our problems, and chart the course toward our higher aspirations. Again, the example of the cat—when a cat wants to be alone, it will jump down and walk away from you, go lie down, and just be by itself. Solitude is a way to satisfy your love and belonging need when it feels too confining. You can love yourself by using the caring habits with yourself.

By ordering children to do something, the parent is doing to the child (frightening), doing for the child (thinking), and not doing with the child. Jim and his father were clients who illustrate the effect of lashing out at your child by yelling at them and ordering them to do things. Orders are great for the military, but the home needs to be a sanctuary from the external control of the real world outside of the home. The home is the one place where the parent can practice and teach the self-control of Choice Theory to their children and thus help them to become responsible and caring adults.

Jim's Story

I had a private client, Jim, who came in with his son, Terry, because Terry was acting out and not doing what Jim wanted. Terry was a sixteen-year-old athlete who was exceptionally talented in soccer. He had just made the state select team for his age group and was in line for a full college scholarship at a local university. The relationship between the two was strained to the point of breaking, if not already broken. I asked Jim what total behavior he found particularly offensive. Jim responded that Terry was not doing well in school and was using drugs. Both of these things were going to keep him from going to college. A college education was very important to Jim. Jim had his master's degree and thought that a college education was necessary for Terry to make his way in the world. I asked Terry what total behavior of his father's that he found to be particularly offensive. Terry responded that his father yelled at him in a threatening manner. I asked if there was anything else that his father did, and he stated that the yelling was the major thing and if he would stop doing that, then he thought things might be better around the house.

Terry said that his father was very strict and wanted things done his way, when he wanted them done. So, I decided to try a little experiment.

I asked Terry to stand up and not to sit back down until I told him to sit. Terry stood up. I then instructed Jim to tell his son to sit down. Jim looked at me in puzzlement and then asked Terry to sit down by saying, "Sit down, son." In his view, he used a pleasant tone. Terry did as I had asked and remained standing. I asked Terry if that was the way his father yelled at him and Terry responded that his father yelled louder than that when ordering him around and he used an angry tone. I then told Jim that Terry was still standing and not obeying what he had told his son to do. Jim took the challenge to see if he could control Terry more than he thought that I was controlling him. (Actually, it was Terry that was in control of the experiment and it was his choice not to sit down as his father had asked.) He told Terry to sit down with a little more force and anger in his voice. Again, Terry said that his father yelled at him louder and remained standing. Again, I bated Jim and pointed out that Terry was still standing. Jim, speaking in a loud voice with more force and anger, commanded Terry to sit down. Terry held his ground and said that his father yelled even louder. By now Jim was beginning to get frustrated and angry with the whole situation and Terry was beginning to enjoy the experiment and his power that he had over his father … This time Jim yelled at Terry and again Terry remained standing with his arms at his side saying only one word, "Louder." He seemed to be really enjoying me put his father through his paces. Finally, Jim shouted in a very harsh and angry tone, "Sit down, NOW!" Jim pointed to the chair and forcefully moved his hand up and down in a motion for Terry to sit down. Terry's reaction was very telling. As soon as Jim shouted, Terry covered up his face and head with his arms as though his father was going to hit him. I asked Terry if his father had ever hit him and he said that he had never been hit in the head, but he had been spanked on the bottom. This illustrated to both Jim and me that shouting at a person can have the same effect as hitting them and that Terry was trying to keep the blows of his father's voice from hitting him by covering up.

I suggested that Jim could consider four elements to see if they improved their relationship. The four elements are trying alternatives to lashing out at Terry; using the caring habits instead of the deadly habits; helping and supporting Terry in school; and helping Terry when he was hurting from the abuse that he had gotten from Jim and the external control world. Even though there had not been any physical or sexual abuse of Terry by Jim, there had been emotional abuse and neglect of Terry's emotional well-being and to a large extent the well-being of the family.

Jim never yelled at Terry again and started to work on their relationship to satisfy the love and belonging needs that are normally satisfied in a father-son relationship. Jim was able to see the damage he was causing to the relationship by his shouting and that it was pushing Terry away from him instead of getting Terry to do as his father wanted. Jim learned that he couldn't control Terry, or anyone other than himself, with that session. When he tried, he only drove people away from him and lessened the relationship. Jim could apply what he learned in all of the close relationships in his life—with his wife, other children, friends, and co-workers, because they were all afraid of Jim's loud and powerful voice.

Alternatives to Lashing out at Your Child

Most good parents realize there is always much more for them to learn about being good parents. In a perfect world, parents would all have boundless energy, patience, tolerance, understanding, and flexibility. But no one is perfect. So it also helps to have a wide variety of practical skills. The next time everyday pressures build up to the point where you feel like lashing out—STOP! Try any of these simple alternatives. You will feel better … and so will your child. Overreaction and inappropriate anger are extremely common in our high-stress society. Look for similar incidents in the past that did not previously provoke the same angry response—you might be over-stressed at this time from other frustrations in your life. When we are angry, we may say things that stick with our children for a long time. Children can become hurt and confused.

If you overreact, offer your kids a heartfelt apology, along with an explanation. This will help your children to learn to talk about feelings and understand human fallibility.

If you do actually blow up at your children, tend to your own needs as described below.

- Take a deep breath ... and another. Then remember you are the adult. Many of our angering reactions are habitual or well established in our behavioral system, and with practice, we can change them. One way of doing this is through breath control. When angering, our breathing often becomes very short and shallow. This deprives the body of needed oxygen. When you feel angering coming on, take a deep breath, then concentrate on breathing slowly and rhythmically. Listen to the air entering your nostrils and lungs. Breathe into the stomach, letting it expand and contract naturally. Feel the life-giving oxygen cleansing your body. With each exhalation, imagine the tension being released. With each inhalation, let your body fill with new life and energy.

- Close your eyes and imagine you are hearing what your child is about to hear. If you do not like hearing what you are going to say and how you are going to say it, then do not say it. This is a form of the ultimate question in use. Yelling may be an effective way to vent frustration, but most children of frequent yellers soon learn to tune it out. The behavior does not change and kids grow hostile. A better method is to stop and ask yourself how you would like being yelled at. You may have to delay action until your anger is under control. Most children respond better to a calm, reasonable request or command.

Save yelling for emergency situations when you really need to get your child's attention: Look out for that car!

- Press your lips together so you cannot speak and count to ten … or better yet, to twenty.

- Put your child in a time-out chair. (Remember the rule: one time-out minute for each year of age up to ten minutes.) Put yourself in a time-out chair, too. Think about why you are angry: is it your child, or is your child simply a convenient target for your anger?

- Phone a friend, talk over the situation, and ask for advice.

- If someone can watch the children, go outside and take a walk.

- Take a hot bath or splash cold water on your face.

- Hug a pillow.

- Turn on some music. Maybe even sing along. Singing opens up the throat and lets the feelings get out of the body.

- Pick up a pencil and write down as many helpful words as you can think of. Save the list.

- When a child asks for your time, attention, or something you can do for them, say yes unless there is a good reason to say no, instead of automatically saying no unless there is a good reason to say yes. This makes the home more positive and active instead of negative and sedentary. Saying yes unless you can think of a good reason to say no takes the large gray area of "I do not really care one way or the other" and puts it into the yes category.

- Try to recognize the sense in your child's behavior. What is the intention behind your child's choice of total behavior? What basic need is your child trying to satisfy? How can you help your child satisfy that need in an acceptable manner? Know your child's development stage and the typical behaviors of that stage. Pre-school children have different behaviors from latency-aged children who have different behaviors from adolescents.

- Favor your love and belonging need over your power need because it will strengthen the relationship between you and your child.

- Encourage your child to generate more effective ways of getting his basic needs met.

- Convey a sense of confidence in your child's own capability to balance his needs and to make responsible choices.

- People don't respond well to demands because they are an expression of external control and they show disrespect. Commands to "Come here this instant!" or "Stop that this second!" are often ignored and tuned out because they push the people apart. A better method of communication is to make a respectful or firm request ... and praise and reward good behavior. Example: When your child gets ready for bed without a fuss, tell him or her, "You got into your pajamas so nicely, I'm going to read you an extra story tonight."

- Nagging is one of the deadly habits and it is often a problem for parents who try to be lenient or permissive. They don't want to get angry but are constantly asking, "Did you clean your room yet?" until they explode. A better way to get the child's full attention is to stand in front of the TV screen rather than calling from another room. Make firm, consistent requests with clear limits. It is very helpful to praise and reward a first-time response. If needed, give a warning ... "Lunch is in twenty minutes." Impose a negative consequence if the task is not completed. "If the garbage is still here, there will be no TV after your homework."

- Lecturing is fruitless. It sounds like criticizing, complaining, and nagging all rolled up into one deadly habit. Children, as well as adults, have a limited attention span for monologues that involve no interaction. And lectures often do not address the problem. For example, lecturing your child about the value of an education when his or her homework is chronically late does not address the home-work issue. It is better to ask questions. "What happens when you do your homework?" "What do you do first?" "Is there a part that you don't understand?"

- Advice is not fruitless, but it is often given when it is not wanted or at the wrong time, and it looks like criticizing. For example, an anxious child who has brought home a poor report card will not be receptive to advice. A positive strategy to reduce the anxiety would be to say something like, "I see you're upset by this. Let's both think of some ways to help your grades, and we'll talk about it after dinner." Other alternatives might be role-playing. "I'll be you, and you'll be your teacher." Teach a coping strategy. "Would you like to know a good way to handle that?" Learn to use informal opportunities to teach a lesson or make a point.

Relaxation will assist you in being able to use the caring habits with your children as well as with others in your life. If you can take the time to relax before responding to a frustrating situation, here is a method that has brought success in many frustrating situations. First, lie or sit in a comfortable position (preferably with loose-fitting clothing) and allow the mind to drift. Then, beginning with the feet, systematically tense and release each muscle in the body. Concentrate on feet, calves, thighs, buttocks, abdomen, back, arms, chest, neck, and face, one muscle group at a time. Then tense the entire body for a few seconds and relax completely. Sink into the chair or melt into the ground. Feel the tension draining away.

A variation of the previous relaxation exercise is to imagine each muscle group becoming very heavy. Repeat in your mind for twenty or thirty seconds, "My right foot is heavy … My right foot is heavy," while imagining it sinking into the floor. Then do the same with the other parts of your body. In time, you will find you can control your feelings to a remarkable degree. The reason for this is that our total behavior is a coordinated choice and we act as we think. The body follows the lead of the mind. If the mind is agitated and troubled, the body is nervous and tense. If the mind is quiet and calm, the body is also tranquil. The total behavior concept states that we can control our thoughts and actions, but our feelings and physiology correspond to those thoughts and actions. Take time out to consult with your inner self because it is a reservoir of strength, peace, and wisdom that can help you deal with the frustrations that you encounter.

These are some of the keys to parenting by Choice Theory. Instead of stopping, suppressing, or controlling behavior, connect with your child through understanding and encouragement. With a strong relationship between you and your child, your child is better prepared to generate new behavior as he or she needs it. Your child can choose better ways to satisfy his or her needs for power, belonging, fun, and freedom.

STOP Using Words that Hurt (Deadly Habits): START Using Words that Help (Caring Habits)

Sticks and stones may break my bones, but words will never hurt me.

Do you remember that childhood chant? Children use it to protect themselves against being hurt when someone is calling them names. It does not work. Words can hurt—and they do. But just as words can hurt, words also can help!

Parents often don't realize they make remarks that cause their children to feel smaller, inadequate, less intelligent or more insecure. An example would be: "Why are you acting like such a baby? That's the dumbest thing you ever said. If you can't behave, I'm leaving forever." It is better to monitor your language and be aware how often you say positive versus negative things. Make sure you are dealing adequately with your own feelings so they don't spill over onto your kids.

Here are some expressions that can give children confidence and raise their self-esteem:

I love you.
That's great!
Let's talk about you.
I believe you can do it.
Believe in yourself as I believe in you.
You're going to be just fine.
You're very special.
Good job.
Yes.

Feeling safe and loved at home is important for children. A parent can help them by letting them know that they are loved and respected. Some of the classic problems that parents have with their children are going to bed, use of the phone, cleaning their room, and the friends that they hang around with in their free time. Choice Theory addresses these problems through the language the parent uses with the child to discuss them. External control is the method that many parents have used in the past and they have had little or no success. A simple change to Choice Theory language can help. Examples of one possible way that parents can respond to these situations are given in *The Language of Choice Theory*, by William and Carleen Glasser (1999). This book gives many more examples that are useful to parents and children. Choice Theory helps to give the people involved the self assurance to maintain dignity when they are dealing with difficult issues in the life of a family. The book gives examples of the language between parent and child, love and marriage, teacher to student, and manager to employee. The following are some examples of parent and child dialogue.

External Control	Choice Theory Alternative
How many times do I have to tell you? Bedtime is nine o'clock! No television tomorrow night if you do not go to bed this minute.	As long as you're quiet and do not disturb anyone, you can go to bed when you get sleepy. But before I get too sleepy, would you like me to read you a story?
Get off that phone right now! I'm serious. I'm just about ready to stop letting you use the phone at all after dinner.	Things with the phone just are not working out. No one can get through. Grandma said she tried for three hours last night. I'm willing to put in call-waiting, but when someone calls I need you to get right off. Can we try that?
Your room's a pigpen. Clean it up or no car this weekend.	Look, I'm at the point where all I want is for you to keep your door closed. But I have to be honest: I'd like you to clean up your room. It bothers me. If you want some help from me, ask and I'll be glad to pitch in. But I'm not going to clean it for you anymore.
If I catch you anywhere near those kids again, you'll be grounded for life. All they ever do is get into trouble.	I'm frightened at the idea of you being out alone with those kids at your age. It is okay if you see them here when I'm home. If I get to know them a little better, I may change my mind. But if you have a better idea, I'll listen. As long as we keep talking, it'll be okay.

Notice that in dealing with a child, the parent needs to be willing to commit time and attention to the child. Spending time with the child is one of the most successful ways that a parent can show the child that they are loved and cared about. While paying attention to the child, the parent is encouraged to use the caring habits instead of the deadly habits. When the child misbehaves, let the child know there is a problem with his or her behavior, and then listen hard and keep quiet.

If the parent can determine which of the basic needs the child is trying to satisfy with his or her behavior, then they can speak to that need when connecting and communicating with the child. Total behavior is chosen to satisfy one or more of our basic needs. Determine which of the basic needs the child is trying to satisfy; try to help him or her satisfy those needs with constructive total behavior. Then the parent will be successful in being *with* the child in his or her choosing of those more constructive total behaviors.

In Chapter V in his book, *The Art of Perfect Parenting and Other Absurd Ideas*, Dr. Yellen (2004) discusses what he calls *Adultisms* and *Ego Boosters*.

> Adultisms are those negative terms, phrases, or ideas that seem to be a part of parent/adult audio tapes of the mind that get replayed to the next generation simply because we once heard them. They are born out of frustration, anger and loss of control on the part of the parent. They serve no constructive purpose and only serve to undermine children's self esteem.

Adultisms are deadly habits based on the concept of external control and angering in the relationship with your child. They are stored in our behavioral system and are acted out automatically with little thought of our total behavior. Yellen continues,

Ego Boosters, on the other hand, make kids, and really all people, feel good about themselves and the decisions they have made. They are an important component in producing healthy, self assured, critical-thinking, sensitive individuals who are not only confident in facing the challenges that await them but have the skills necessary to be successful most of the time. A few of these comments, well-placed, will prove fantastic [results].

Choice Theory describes Ego Boosters as caring habits and claims the same benefits as Dr. Yellen in the raising of your children. Changing the behavioral system to include these caring habits requires practice and forethought. It does not come overnight, but does come with constant awareness and practice.

Helping Your Child Be Successful at School

School-age children often spend more time with their teachers than they do with their parents. It is important that the parents, the children, and the teachers have a good working relationship. A good relationship will help children do better in school as well as reduce stress in the family life. Again, here is an example of the language of external control and the Choice Theory alternative from *The Language of Choice Theory* (1999) that will help children be successful at school.

External Control	Choice Theory Alternative
Do your homework now. I do not care what it is. You have to do it or no TV tonight.	Okay, I'm not going to argue with you. Let's look that homework over together to see if you understand it. And I'll be right here to help you if you get stuck.

In his books, *The Quality School* (1998), *Choice Theory in the Classroom* (2001), and *Every Student Can Succeed* (2004), Dr. Glasser explains how schools can create quality education for students. Dr. Glasser has established six criteria for his Quality Schools.

The six criteria from *Every Student Can Succeed* are:

1. Relationships are based upon trust and respect, and all discipline problems, not incidents, have been eliminated.
2. Total Learning Competency is stressed and an evaluation that is below competence, what is now a "B," has been eliminated. All schooling has been replaced by useful education.
3. All students do some quality work each year that is significantly beyond competence. All such work receives an "A" grade or higher, such as an "A+".
4. Students and staff are taught to use Choice Theory in their lives and in their work in school. Parents are encouraged to participate in study groups to become familiar with the ideas of Dr. Glasser.
5. Students do better on state proficiency tests and college entrance examinations. The importance of these tests is emphasized in the school.
6. Staff, students, parents, and administrators view the school as a joyful place.

If a child is not lucky enough to be in one of the few Glasser Quality Schools, *Every Student Can Succeed* explains how to reach and teach every student in the public schools. And *Choice Theory in the Classroom* is a book for use by teachers who would like to experience the joy of teaching children to succeed without punishment. When teachers read both these books and put the information into practice, the children's experience in the classroom is enhanced.

Here are some ideas for building a relationship of trust with children and their teachers:

- Be aware of difficulties. If you learn about a problem, investigate as soon as possible. Listen to both sides. (Many parents believe that the teacher is always right, and many parents believe that the child is always right.) Keep an open mind.
- Talk to your child about daily events at school.
- Be involved in homework. Find out if your child's teacher regularly assigns homework.
- Make sure your child has a quiet place to work. After dinner, the kitchen table can be a good place to study.
- Establish a routine at home. Set up regular times to complete homework, play, and go to bed.

If your child brings home a disappointing report card:

- Sit down with your child and look over the report card.
- Praise your child. Find at least one good thing on the report card: attendance, no tardiness.
- Be calm! Let your child tell you about his or her poor grades.
- Ask how you can help your child do better.
- Ask what your child can do to make better grades.
- Make a plan with your child's teacher and your child to do better.

The Parent Outreach California program of California Institute on Human Services at Sonoma State University has developed a mnemonic of parenting tips using the word PARENTS. It provides seven tips that support Choice Theory's view of parenting.

Praise good behavior and accomplishments.

Ask a trusted friend or family member for assistance. Schedule regular breaks for yourself.

Relax. When angry, count to ten or take five minutes to cool down.

Enjoy time with your child. Turn off the TV. Play a game, do an activity, take a walk.

Nurture your child's judgment; let him or her make choices and decisions when appropriate.

Talk to your child about your family's values and important rules. Be consistent.

Stop misbehavior by distracting the child with a positive activity and choices.

PART II

REALITY THERAPY APPLICATION

CHAPTER 7

Introduction

This part of the book illustrates the use of Choice Theory and Reality Therapy in a group setting for individuals who are batterers of other family members or are violent in the home or community. This section can be helpful to those who have a difficult time dealing with their angering total behavior as a means of combating their feeling of powerlessness in an external control world. The example used is a man who is separated from his family and who is attending domestic violence groups as ordered by the courts. The process is not limited to this example, but is usable for individual and group counseling, for parenting education, and for individual application in a self-help manner.

Some Basics of Reality Therapy

The purpose of all behavior in Reality Therapy is to mold the external world to match inner pictures or wants. Clients seek counseling because their behavior is ineffective in molding that external world and thus they are in pain. They sometimes want the therapist to help them find a new way to control, or mold, the world. Ironically, it is this precise goal that is most difficult to achieve directly, for it is almost impossible to change the external world. A paradox occurs when clients change their wants or their own behavioral systems; paradoxically, their external world often subsequently changes. When abusers and aggressors learn to stop criticizing their spouses or children, they are often pleasantly surprised to find that their spouses' or children's behavior changes as well. On the other hand, the more the abusers push, the greater is the resistance from the spouse or child. In attempting to change only those elements over which the client has control, the environment in which they live also changes.

Relationship is the key to Choice Theory. The relationship between each group member and the facilitator is a model for them to use in their lives outside of the group room. The facilitator tries to model the following eight steps with the clients in an attempt to help them choose non-violent behavior and the caring habits over violent behavior and the deadly habits. By living the model in the group, the client can begin to trust in a positive caring relationship. The facilitator may not always be successful at being a perfect example, but the attempt is the model itself.

1. Create a friendly relationship and get involved with the client.
2. Focus on the current behavior of the client.
3. Encourage the client to evaluate his own total behavior.
4. Have the client develop an action plan.
5. Have the client commit to the action plan.
6. Refuse to accept excuses and minimization by the client.
7. Refuse to punish the client for not knowing or using the caring habits.
8. Refuse to give up on the client.

A successful facilitator needs the personal qualities of empathy, congruence, and positive regard. The facilitator needs to be energetic in group and not give up on the clients. She or he (I'll use the pronoun "he", since I am basing this description on my own practice.) must have the ability to see things as an advantage without getting discouraged or being a Pollyanna about situations. The facilitator must have a positive, but not naïve, view of human nature and the legal systems. He must have a sense of paradox and metaphors for use with the clients along with the ability to communicate hope and to define a problem in solvable terms. He must be willing to work within the boundaries of professional guidelines, standards, and ethics, and must be culturally sensitive toward the clients.

The group room that I use has posters and diagrams on the wall illustrating the principles of Choice Theory. These remind the client of the concepts and terminology that is being used. I often refer to the posters during the discussions. One of the posters lists the ten axioms of Choice Theory, and we refer to them regularly to remind the clients of the limitations of their influence on others. When a client attempts to bring in external control concepts to expand their or someone else's control over another, someone in the group will gently remind the client of the axiom that he has forgotten. I also give each client a copy of a condensed version of *Angering in the Family* so that he can have the basics to refer to when he is away from the group.

Group Dynamics

Domestic violence groups have established some guidelines that make the discussion more free-flowing and satisfy the California Probation Department's rules for accreditation. They start with the mandates from the court, which state that if a client misses more than three weekly sessions, the absences must be reported to the court. The facility cannot determine which absences are excusable and which are not. The facility cannot allow make-up of missed sessions. The office requires the client to call before the class if he is going to be absent, or else they charge him for the missed session. This places the responsibility on the client to either attend the group or call the office. The court also requires the sessions to be one-hundred ten minutes long. Since we schedule one-hundred twenty minutes (two hours) between groups, it is up to the group to establish if they get a ten-minute smoke break in the middle or end the group ten minutes before the next one starts. Most groups elect the ten-minute break in the middle even if they do not smoke; they can go to the toilet or just talk. To eliminate confusion as to the start and stop time, my watch is designated as the master clock. This is one of the few external controls that are placed on the groups, but we have found that, this way, there are no diversions in discussions as to when a client is late or whether we should take a break or end the group. Cell phones and pagers are to be turned off during the sessions.

We, the group, ask the group members to be considerate of each other and not to talk or hold side discussions while someone else is talking. We look for positive feedback from group members instead of bashing of other people or the system. The clients are allowed their own opinions of the system without fear of being reported to the authorities, but complaints are followed by constructive ways to use the system as an aid to satisfying their five basic needs. There are times when members of the legal community, i.e., law enforcement, judges, or lawyers are reported not to have performed their duties as clients thought that they should. These things happen in the real world, and the clients need to learn how to deal with the frustration these issues can cause.

It is important for the clients to be open and honest about their relationships and what goes on in their lives during the week, so we follow a very thin line between what they report and what really occurred. The court mandates the facilitator to report any violation of any law or any contact with law enforcement by a person on probation. If a client tells the facilitator that he was stopped by law enforcement for speeding, the facilitator is mandated to inform the client's probation officer or the court. This mandate inhibits discussion of many of the less serious violations of the law that we could discuss to determine better ways of handling. I am not a student of the law and cannot know every time a law has been broken, but I do draw a very distinct line when it comes to acting out their frustrations with their woman friends or children. They cannot report that they got into a physical argument with the spouse and yelled at her because, not only does it cross my line, but also it is considered another violation of the domestic violence laws. If a client cannot bring up an issue without the fear of being reported, how can we deal with real-life issues that are not just made up situations? I, therefore, allow them to use "what if" preceding their reports of anything that might be reportable to the court as a violation of probation. In this manner, a client can bring to the discussion situations that are more realistic and the group can help him learn how to deal with them in the future without resorting to elevating the level of anger. Real-life situations are more constructive in the learning process than ones that are made up by a group member or me.

Finally, my agency allows and invites those group members who complete the court-mandated sessions to return, free of charge, to discuss any issues that may arise after they graduate. Group members take us up on this offer and bring many practical experiences to be discussed in the group. They have commented that it helps them deal with problems of a personal nature and provides a safe place to discuss those problems with the group and facilitator in order to gain resolution and happiness.

The key to changing the pattern of aggressive conduct is self-evaluation and awareness. As with any important behavioral change, this occurs only when the person exhibiting the behavior becomes impressed that it is essentially self-defeating and resolves to try a new behavior. Aggressive people are typically not very reflective and often seem insensitive to self-examination. They find it too challenging and even painful to consider that they are perpetuating their own problems and difficulties. Punishment, external control, is not a very effective method to increase the aggressor's self-awareness. Instead, punishment encourages more anger and aggressive behavior. With the tools of Choice Theory, they can find better ways to satisfy their basic needs through non-aggressive total behavior.

Group therapy as described in Wubbolding, *Reality Therapy for the Twenty-first Century* (2000), has four stages, initial, transitional, working, and termination. In the initial stage, the facilitator addresses the need for belonging so that everyone feels included in the group. Each client is asked what he wants out of the group, what his life direction is, specific actions, ineffective and effective self-talk, feelings, and even physiological behaviors. Since the domestic violence groups are revolving groups and a new one does not start each week or when a new member comes to the agency, the need for belonging is addressed for each new member on his first meeting in the group. The new member is told the rules and guidelines, which reviews them for the older members, and the new member is asked to describe the event for which he was arrested and sentenced to the group. In this way, he tells his personal story. Many times, he minimizes his behavior or denies doing anything wrong, but this is addressed by going over the definitions of family aggression and showing him how he is included in the definition. Minimal acceptance by the client is a start to addressing his aggressive tendency to try to control others.

The first client I had when I started facilitating domestic violence groups said that he was court-ordered to the group because he had "kind of pushed" his wife and the police came and arrested him.

The transitional stage described by Wubbolding (2000) addresses the power need of the client when anxiety, conflict, and resistance to the concepts arise. The facilitator uses his skills of the caring habits of supporting, encouraging, listening, accepting, trusting, respecting, and negotiating the differences, to develop a caring relationship with the client. Again, since the group is a revolving group, this is done throughout the entire time that the client is in the group. As group members become stronger in their commitment to Choice Theory and non-violent or non-aggressive behavior, they support the newer members of the group by use of the caring habits, too. This is pointed out by the facilitator as evidence of member maturity.

After a few months, this first client admitted that he had actually "body slammed" his wife while they were having an argument. This client was beginning to develop a relationship of trust with me and the other group members. He began to believe that no one in the group would think the worst of him, because he had heard others admit that they had been very violent with their mates.

In the third stage, the working stage, love and belonging is addressed. Wubbolding (2000) addresses this "when the group members come to believe that others in the group can be of some help to them." Wubbolding states, "The central importance of this phase is illustrated by the emphasis given by the therapist to helping group members evaluate the various aspects of their own control systems: wants, levels of commitment, and total behavior." He continues, "At this stage therapists ask group members to assist each other in making self-evaluations." In the revolving group, this occurs at each meeting. The people who have been in the group longer confront the statements and behavior that do not seem to be consistent with the caring habits. It is this confrontation that the facilitator must monitor to maintain a caring community for the less experienced members. Monitoring of each member's activity during the past week brings up topics that need to be addressed. In some sessions, the topic of one member takes the entire group time and all members are encouraged to participate in the discussion with their ideas, suggestions, and opinions. The entire discussion is summarized as the seventh axiom of Choice Theory which states, "All we can give or get from other people is information. How we deal with that information is our or their choice." One of the major differences between Reality Therapy and Choice Theory and other therapeutic interventions is that the facilitator is not telling or directing the clients how to behave. The facilitator gives information and asks the client to consider it to see if the information will better satisfy his basic needs. If the client accepts the information, he is asked to establish a plan to implement his use of the information. Progress on the plan is then monitored on a weekly basis.

Wubbolding's (2000) final stage is the termination stage. In it, further planning helps address the fun and belonging needs in addition to touching on the freedom or autonomy needs. The revolving group addresses these needs throughout the normal sessions when a member is coming to the end of his court-ordered time in the group. Most of the group members experienced a loss of freedom when they went to jail for their crime. Additionally, for the duration of the time in group and during their community service, their free time and money has been taken from them. A question that is addressed during the sessions is, "Was your behavior worth the price you had to pay in freedom of time and money?" The answer is always "NO!" Many clients state that what they learned from the groups was worth the time and money spent, but they wish that they could have done it without all of the court intervention. They do admit that they would not have taken the class if it were not mandated by an external control force.

In the last session of the group for my first client, he stated that not only had he "body slammed" his wife, but he had to take her to the hospital to have eight stitches in her head because she had hit it on the coffee table when he threw her to the floor. This client had been able to accept that his behavior had been dangerous toward his wife and that he had come close to killing her by his actions. To admit to and accept that his behavior could have been deadly was a large step for this client. The client was able to make a plan for his future behavior and make a high level of commitment to non-violent behavior in the future.

External Control vs. Choice Theory

External control is used by most of the civilized world in an attempt to maintain an orderly society. The key word is *orderly* and it is defined by those in control of the rest of the people. External control is externally motivated and realities are the same for everyone. It is based on the premise that those in power can control others, that events control the person instead of the person controlling events, that coercion is best to get others to follow the rules, and that it is a win/lose proposition for all. External control leads to the feeling of powerlessness that leads to frustration and

EXTERNAL CONTROL vs. CHOICE THEORY

- **Externally motivated**
- **Realities the same**
- **Can control others**
- **Events control me**
- **Coercion**
- **Win / Lose**

- **Internally motivated**
- **Realities different**
- **Can only control self**
- **Events just happen**
- **Collaboration**
- **Win / Win**

then to anger, hostility, and ultimately violence. When someone in our world is not providing satisfying total behavior, the control imperative suggests that we try harder to change him or her. They do not like it, and they tend to push back. The harder we try, the harder they push back until the relationship is broken and the people distance themselves from one another.

Arun Gandhi, the grandson of Mahatma Gandhi of India, gave an excellent example of external control and Choice Theory at the 2006 International Conference on Violence, Abuse, and Trauma. He asked each member of the audience to choose a partner and for one of them to close their fist as though holding a very valuable diamond. He asked the other to try to open the fist to get the diamond. Almost all of the members of the audience tried to force the hand with the diamond open using one technique or another. A few asked their partner to open the fist and give them the diamond. Those who tried to force the fist open were using external control and those who asked their partner to open the fist used Choice Theory and the caring habits with their partner—they gave the partner the choice of relinquishing the diamond or not.

Violence is used in an attempt to get others to do what the aggressor wants them to do. Violence is used throughout the world in an attempt to control others. It is like saying, "I know what is best for you and I'll force you to do things my way so that I can be happy because you cannot be happy unless I am happy." I ask the members when they first join the group if they like the judge controlling them and making them take this group. I have yet to get an affirmative answer. Then I ask them, "Do you think that anyone else likes for you to control them?" I tell them that I will provide them with some information and let them make up their minds what they want to do with it. I will not force them to make any changes if they do not want to make them.

Experts say jailing abusers will not stop the violence or solve the family aggression problem in the community. They note that, without treatment, abusers will continue the cycle of violence and will probably wind up back behind bars. External control proponents believe that success in most of the batterers' programs stems from the batterer's fear that something—his wife, family, or home—will be taken away. It is those people who do not care about what they might lose who are the most difficult to treat. Choice Theory proponents believe that Choice Theory can be taught to all aggressive people with success.

Choice Theory as differentiated from external control teaches the following:

- That we are internally motivated,
- That our realities are different from each other,
- That we can only control our individual self,
- That events just happen and we have choices on how to react to them,
- That we maintain an orderly relationship with collaboration,
- That Choice Theory is a win/win proposition for all people.

Choice Theory places the responsibility of orderly conduct on the individual and the therapy teaches him how to make decisions that will meet his basic needs without infringing on the basic needs and happiness of others. Choice Theory leads to self-reliance, internal power and control, choice of one's actions, and ultimately, to happiness and internal peace.

The language of Choice Theory is used in the groups. It is important because it reframes the thoughts of external control and of powerlessness into that of inner control and empowerment. Some examples of the change in language are given below:

External Control	Choice Theory
I cannot.	I choose not to. Or I will not.
He made me do it.	I chose to do it.
You do not give me any choice.	I do not see that I do not have any choices.
My parents will not let me …	I choose to do what my parents want.
I cannot stand it.	I chose not to tolerate it and left the area.
A fit of depression came over me.	I chose to depress.
I had an anxiety attack.	I chose to be anxious.
He makes me sick.	I choose to be sick when I am around him.
This rain gets me down.	I choose to depress when we have rain.
She really gets to me.	I choose to get upset regarding her actions.
My job is stressful.	I choose to react with stress over my job.
This situation upsets me.	I choose to get upset over this situation.
My child is such a worry to me.	I choose to worry over my child's behavior.
You did not tell me.	I did not know.
That kid drives me up the wall.	I get upset with that child's behavior.

Just reading the Choice Theory statements, the reader may feel better about the way things are stated. The statements tend to give one a sense of empowerment and self control.

Domestic Violence or Family Aggression Defined

Here are some guidelines that Los Angeles City law enforcement uses in determining if domestic violence has occurred and who the aggressor is:

The *dominant aggressor* is the *most significant*, not necessarily the first, aggressor.

The officer shall consider:

- Intent of the law to protect domestic violence victims
- Threats creating fear of domestic violence
- History of domestic violence between the two
- If either acted in self-defense
- Presence of fear
- Credibility
- Offensive/defensive injuries
- Seriousness of injuries
- Corroborating evidence
- Height of parties
- Weight of parties
- Use of drugs/alcohol
- Amount of detail in statement
- Level of violence
- Criminal history
- Existing court orders (past and/or present)

Domestic violence is considered a felony if one of the parties is injured. If the law enforcement officer did not witness the violence, he or she can make an arrest for an assault based on probable cause. This is based upon locating and evaluating evidence such as statements of the parties, statements of witnesses, behavior of the parties, physical evidence at the scene, and injuries to the parties.

When I served on a jury, the judge defined battery as "touching a person, their clothing, or immediate possessions while you are angry." The definition does not include a description of any injury—just *touching*.

Wendy Patrick Mazzarella, deputy district attorney for San Diego County, defines abuse as intentionally or recklessly causing or trying to cause bodily injury or putting another person in fear of serious bodily injury. For abuse to be domestic violence, it must be done to a spouse, former spouse, cohabitant, former cohabitant, co-parent, or partner in a dating or engagement relationship.

The judicial branch sometimes uses the domestic violence groups in cases that involve anger management or where the bench believes that anger management counseling would be of benefit to the client. Choice Theory and Reality Therapy is applicable to both domestic violence and anger management groups in addition to parenting groups.

The above information is discussed when the client comes to the group so that he may get an understanding of why the court mandated him to attend a group. This discussion usually reduces the resentment of the client for being court-ordered to the group. It also allows the client to accept the ruling by being included in the "just touching" category. Most clients will admit to touching their partners while they were angry, even though they claim their partners hit them also.

Can abusers be cured, or must they be punished?

A quiet battle is brewing among those who work with batterers over what type of treatment will best protect the victims of family violence. This treatment debate stems from a deeper schism over what makes batterers tick. The family violence issue has been distorted and politicized by the gender wars. Believing what gender activists say about family violence is like believing what tobacco companies say about cancer. Unfortunately, almost all information available to the public comes in the form of political propaganda from men's rights groups or women's rights groups. There is some truth to both sides, but not all truth to either.

This misunderstanding of the family violence issue is so pervasive that city and county governments, the courts, law enforcement, prosecutor's offices, mental health clinics, and other tax-supported agencies are now funding programs based on gender politics rather than on responsible scientific studies. There are more than one hundred solid scientific studies that reveal a startlingly different picture of family violence than those we usually see in the media.

Scientific data shows that both men and women are violent to a far greater extent than police statistics reveal. This scientific data shows that spousal violence is mostly unreported. In fact, some degree of violence occurs at a rate of one-hundred thirteen incidents per one thousand couples per year (husband on wife) and one-hundred twenty-one incidents per thousand couples per year (wife on husband).

Domestic violence is violence which takes place at home, the word *domestic* referring to the definition "of or relating to the household or the family." Female violence against children is another taboo topic among gender activists.

On one side is the pro-feminist approach—maintaining that family abuse is the product of a sexist society that accepts male dominance over women. Many men have been taught to view women as sex objects—a woman is a man's property and it is both his right and his duty as a man to dominate. This position maintains that men do not respect women and what needs to change is that sense of entitlement—that it is their right to control the lives of their partners. Battering is not a sickness, it is a learned behavior. The pro-feminists view power and control as the driving force behind family aggression, which is consistent with this line of reasoning. Batterers are control freaks who consciously manipulate their partners to ensure they get their way. Men need to be told by women how to act or be thrown in jail.

On the other side of the debate is the psychological model. This side believes that violence stems from deep character flaws created by traumatic childhood experiences and stunted character development. Following this line of thinking, the best way to protect women is to explore, and ultimately change, the glaring character defects that drive the abuser. At the core of this treatment battle is a debate over whether batterers can change.

Based on their belief that batterers are fundamentally controlling, calculating, manipulative people, the pro-feminist thinkers believe this is a pie-in-the-sky hope. As a result, these pro-feminist/behavior modification programs employ a social control approach to batterers' treatment that focuses almost exclusively on the here and now. Group leaders confront the batterers, forcing them to accept responsibility for their actions. They are not allowed to blame their behavior on their partner, alcohol, the economy, their temper, their childhood, or any other excuse. They did it, there was no excuse—and they either will stop or they will be put in jail. Group members explore the attitudes toward women they use to justify their abuse. They learn ways to control their anger, and communicate more effectively with their partners. They learn that abuse is not just beatings, but also threats, insults, psychological abuse, and economic control.

There has been an ongoing debate between the psychological and the confrontational, external control approach and there still is not any conclusion. But there is no doubt that men who come to batterer programs are like long-term alcoholics—they have developed tremendous systems of rationalization and denial and need a strong, clear, and consistent message. The more you diffuse that message with psychology, the more it feeds into their rationalization. The sooner they accept responsibility for their behavior, the sooner their victims will be safe.

Richard Gelles, a nationally recognized domestic violence researcher at the University of Rhode Island, said there is no evidence that the confrontational method works best in all cases. Belief that it does is based more on what makes the treatment professional feel good than on any empirical evidence.

While incorporating many of the principles and methods developed in the pro-feminist approach, proponents of the psychological model believe the only way to protect women is to help the men change. They believe that if you want to make the effects of treatment last, you have to make these men change from the inside out. If all you do is threaten them with the court and jail, it will not last. The pro-feminist views all batterers as calculating criminals.

The Choice Theory model that is described in this book combines the pro-feminist and the psychological models and addresses elements from both points of view. It teaches the batterers that they cannot control others; that they are responsible for all of their total behavior; and that external control can be replaced by internal control (Choice Theory) that will bring them happiness and peace in their present relationships.

Most of these men are not proud of what they are doing and a lot of their resistance to treatment is in not wanting to face the shame of what they have done. We try to foster pride in dealing with a situation in a way that shows respect for the partner and stresses their responsibility for their total behavior. A large portion of the program is spent helping batterers build their ability to make better decisions and use the caring habits instead of the deadly habits.

Those who favor the pro-feminist/behavioral approach contend that allowing batterers to explore their inner wounds undermines the hard-won gains of the first half of the treatment. Choice Theory believes that the pain that happened in the past has a great deal to do with who we are today; however, revisiting the past pain can contribute little or nothing to what we need to do now: improve an important, present relationship. This is a behavioral education program that teaches Choice Theory to the client.

There is no research to support the notion that short-term therapy works. The fifty-two weeks of the mandated program is long enough for all but the most ingrained men to endorse and begin to use the tenets of Choice Theory. Only a small percentage of the men coming through the program are macho control freaks that are unable to make the choice to change their behavior and improve their happiness through an improved important relationship. This program teaches the client how to make such a change.

Requirements to Close a Court Case

When aggression comes to the attention of the courts, the following conditions are considered by the court prior to deciding on the need for further counseling or case closure. The court uses the word *defendant* to identify the *primary aggressor* who was established by law enforcement investigation. The primary aggressor is the person who elevated the violence to a level intended to control the other person. This does not mean that the partner was not also an aggressor, but the partner is considered the *victim* by the courts. The defendant is often the male aggressor in the relationship because the male is the one who is able to elevate the level of physical violence to one that could be used to control the behavior of his partner. In other words, the male is the one who can overpower the female in most relationships.

There are eight stated requirements to close a case in the courts of California:

1. The defendant has been violence-free for a minimum of one year. This includes all forms of violence including violence outside of an intimate relationship.
2. The defendant has cooperated and participated in the batterers' program.

3. The defendant demonstrates an understanding of and practices positive conflict resolution skills.

4. The defendant does not blame, degrade, or has not committed acts that dehumanize the victim or puts the victim's safety at risk.

5. The defendant understands that the use of coercion or violent behavior to maintain dominance is unacceptable in an intimate relationship.

6. The defendant has not made threats to harm anyone in any manner. Again, this includes behavior outside of the intimate relationship.

7. The defendant has complied with applicable requirements to receive alcohol and/or drug counseling.

8. The defendant demonstrates acceptance of responsibility for the abusive behavior perpetrated against the victim.

Rachor (1995) used self-reports from both men and women to evaluate the first step in the Passages Domestic Violence Program. Even though the study was flawed by inadequate controls as well as by participants who underreported their aggression, the study still showed notable results. Comparable studies cited by Rachor indicated that many other treatment programs seldom made any difference in recidivism, while some studies indicated modest decreases in violence.

The clients, men and women, participated in a twenty-one-session program, subdivided into two phases, with each session lasting two and a half hours. The first phase dealt with the application of Choice Theory and Reality Therapy to family aggression as well as to the roots of family aggression, cycles of violence, and related topics. The second phase consisted of applying the techniques to the family as units, to help children. For example, clients worked on developing an internal locus of control and encouraging all family members to spend quality time in relationships.

People who think they have no control over events and situations, who believe that they are victims of what happens around them, have an *external locus of control.* They believe that they are controlled by external events and other people. People who believe that they always have alternatives in the way they respond to events and other people, regardless of the circumstances, have an *internal locus of control.* They know that external events influence them, but do not control their choices. They know they can choose different approaches to deal with events they cannot control.

This survey research included forty-five clients (twenty-three females and twenty-two males) who were selected randomly. Participants answered open-ended questions via telephone interviews conducted by trained volunteers. The answers were analyzed and grouped under descriptive headings.

Two-thirds of the males reported they learned better self-control and 40 percent of the women indicated increased self-confidence and self-esteem as well as the ability to relinquish attempts to control others. Continued threats of violence were reported by only 17 percent of females, including 13 percent who indicated multiple acts of violence.

Currently California requires one-hundred four hours of mandatory group counseling with the aggressor and has an additional free optional program for the victim. There is no provision for the family to deal with the issues that are the basis for the frustration in the relationship or the effects on the children from the union. I do not know of any studies that have been conducted on the effectiveness of the current California requirements or the use of Choice Theory in a program to accomplish the requirements to close a case. A few men have returned to the program since the institution of Choice Theory, but the returning men report the use of alcohol during the episode or the use of violence in situations outside of the family. Alcohol acts as a mask to the cognitive thinking process of the person, and without deeply imbedded total behaviors in dealing with frustration, the person often reverts back to older actions without thinking about the ultimate question or the consequences that will be imposed by the real world.

Reality Therapy and Choice Theory, as described by Dr. William Glasser in his book *Choice Theory* (1998), allows the aggressor to change the anger into productive choices from destructive choices that are directed against the victims or society. Choice Theory states that we choose our total behavior to fulfill one or more of the basic needs that are a construct of our genetic and our psychological structure. A program using Choice Theory can satisfy all of the requirements listed above so that the court can close the case.

Choice Theory explains the whole mechanism of genetic needs, the symptoms associated with their frustration, and the choices of behavior people make while experiencing their frustration.

The aggressors are responsible for their total behavior. All we can do is give information to others. We explain to the clients that the heart of Reality Therapy and Choice Theory is the message: *The behavior we choose in a relationship, not what the behavior chosen for us or by us for others, is the heart of living happily with another person.*

The facilitator helps the client relate to the individuals in the group as well as to the facilitator. The client can choose to use what he learns with the group and begin to relate more effectively to the other people in his life. The facilitator's interactions set the example so that the client learns how to behave with others by imitating the facilitator's actions, words, and the manner in which he relates to each of the members of the group.

When there is difficulty in any relationship, it is caused by one or both of the parties using external power and control. When we replace that external control with Choice Theory, life will improve. Using Choice Theory in an external control environment—court-ordered mandatory attendance—is a challenging endeavor, but one which can bring great rewards to the family and the community.

CHAPTER 8

Group Reality Therapy Example

I will use a particular situation of one of the group members to illustrate the interaction between the clients and the facilitator. Mike's story provides the framework for this example. Each client is encouraged to take his or her story, go through the process that Mike went through, and respond to the questions in their own manner just as Mike did. This helps them to apply Choice Theory to their situation, realize some alternative total behaviors, and develop plans for their lives when they complete the class.

Mike's counseling occurs in a group setting with up to fifteen clients in the session. Most of the clients are court-ordered to be in group for fifty-two weeks and come to the group with resentment about the external control that sent them there. When Mike first came to the group, he minimized and even denied the violence of his behavior and the stressful events that led to his making the choice to use violence against his domestic partner. It is very difficult for a man to talk in front of a group of strangers and tell them what he did in beating up a woman. Mike knew that he had done something for which he was ashamed and he could not brag about hitting a woman or frightening her so much that she did not want him around her or their child. A significant number of clients were under the influence of drugs or alcohol when they committed the crime, but Mike was not using at the time of the incident. Those clients who were under the influence often state that they cannot remember what happened. This is a way of avoiding the reality of their actions.

Mike is a big man, six feet tall, two-hundred seventy-five pounds, with a shaved head and a few tattoos on his arms. He has already completed one court-ordered domestic violence program that was based on an external control model that attacked the men and their way of thinking without giving them positive reinforcement and goals. He was separated from Judy, his girlfriend and the mother of his three-year-old child, because of his acting out in threatening manners. They separated with Mike's understanding that it is a trial of whether they can get back together without living together. Mike was married previously and when that marriage dissolved due to his violent behavior, he lost custody of his child by that woman. His ex-wife has obtained permission from the court to allow her to move away from Mike. The court also ordered Mike to have monitored visits with the child. Mike is unable to visit very often because there is no one in the town where his ex-wife lives who will monitor his visits; therefore, he must bring someone from Los Angeles with him. Since his ex-wife lives about three hundred miles away from Los Angeles, it is virtually impossible for Mike to arrange a visit.

One day Mike went to Judy's apartment and found another man there. This man's psychotropic medicine was on the table where Mike's daughter could get to it. The apartment was on the second floor and the front door was the only normal entrance or exit. Mike looked at the apartment through the window and judged that the apartment was dirty and messy and he thought that this was a threat to his daughter's health and safety. (The condition of the apartment had been one of the issues that he and Judy had fought about and which led to her asking him to move out.) Mike entered the apartment using his key. Judy and the man took one look at Mike, retreated to her bedroom, and locked the door. Mike looked to be very angry and in a rage. Mike kicked the bedroom door open and entered the room. The man was frightened by Mike's appearance, went to the bedroom balcony, and jumped over the balcony to get away from Mike. Mike told Judy that he was only going to *talk* with the man, but his facial expression and body language indicated that he was extremely angry. Judy was frightened and called the police. Mike was arrested and charged with vandalism due to the broken door. He was not charged with domestic violence because he did not strike anyone or make any threats to harm anyone. Mike was ordered to take fifty-two more weeks of domestic violence counseling for his actions because the court saw the incident as an act of violence.

This chapter follows the diagram in Chapter Four labeled "Choice Theory—Why and How We Behave" in organization. It deals with each of the elements as they apply to Mike's understanding of his needs, beliefs, perceptions, and total behavior.

Basic Needs

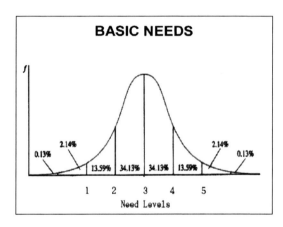

For this model, we will consider that the brain consists of two parts, the cerebral cortex and the part that is considered the reptilian brain. The cerebral cortex contains all conscious and voluntary need-satisfying behavior, and the reptilian part of the brain is used for automatically monitoring the basic need of survival. Psychological needs arise in the cerebral cortex.

The fundamentals of human motivation are derived from five basic needs—*survival, love and belonging, power, freedom,* and *fun.* Like intelligence, these needs are genetic. The choices we make are the ways in which we satisfy them. The level of these needs does not change throughout a person's life, but the manner in which each need is met or addressed does change. Health and happiness come from meeting the basic needs through involvement with others. Each of us has a strength level for each need. The total population has a distribution similar to that of our intelligence quotient—a standard normal curve. A similarity in the strength of each and all of the needs is important for a lasting relationship. Assuming a standard deviation of one rating point, Dr. William and Carleen Glasser, in their book *Getting Together and Staying Together* (2000), suggest that a relationship will have difficulties in the need area if there is difference greater than one rating point in the need category. The clients are encouraged to determine the strength of their own needs to form a basis of establishing a stable relationship with a partner and to understand themselves, their needs and their wants.

On a scale from one (1) to five (5), then on the normal curve pictured, three (3) would be average and 68 percent of the people would fall between two (2) and four (4), and 96 percent of the people would fall on the scale from one (1) and five (5). Two percent would fall below the level of one (1^-) and 2 percent would fall above the level of five (5^+). The nearer that a need level falls to average level of three (3), the more people will fall within +/−1. The closer a need level is to the ends of the curve, one (1) or five (5), the fewer number of people there are who will be compatible with it.

The first of these needs, survival, is a biological need that we share with all living creatures. Love and belonging, freedom, and fun are also shared with the animal kingdom. Power is the uniquely human psychological need. Humans will choose total behavior that is destructive to others in order to satisfy their power need in an external manner. Other animals will not. We differ from one another in the relative strength of our needs, but we all have the same needs. We cannot change or control the basic needs that motivate us, but we can control our choice of specific behaviors to satisfy those needs. We always choose a total behavior that we hope will satisfy one or more of our basic needs.

For each of the needs listed below, I have selected statements among the examples that were written in *Getting Together and Staying Together*.

Every reader can select his or her own items from this book and answer by himself or herself.

This profile is a subjective measure. If you wish, you are more than welcome to correct what you have done and do it again. The most important thing is that the more you understand your profile and your partner's profile, the more you can understand the relationship you are sharing with your partner now. Dr Glasser recommends thinking subjectively about your own needs and your partner's needs that can influence your marital life in many aspects.

To use these statements to determine the individual needs, each client is asked to select the number (Never = 1; Seldom = 2; Sometimes = 3; Often = 4; Always = 5) that most closely represents his total behavior for each statement. Then the client adds the numbers for the ten statements and records the total. Finally, he divides the total by ten to yield the need level indicated in the above figure.

Back to Mike and Judy: I asked Mike to look at the basic needs and to review them for possible application to his situation. He took several minutes and then stated that he was ready to go ahead. Mike had to determine his need levels so that he could determine the importance of each need to himself and his happiness. We will look at the level of Mike's needs as we look at each need category.

Survival

The need for survival and physical well-being drives our healthy behavior. The elements of survival are food, shelter, safety, and reproduction. Reproduction is included as an element of survival because it is the basic element in the survival of the species and this is an extremely strong drive in our lives. The strength of this drive may vary with age and sex, but it is always a part of our reptilian brain.

The following ten statements helped Mike determine his level of survival.

1. I am frugal.
2. Impulsive or reckless spending concerns me.
3. Staying in good health is very important.
4. I try to keep balanced diet.
5. I have a large interest in sex.
6. I am conservative in many aspects.
7. I am saving or investing money for the stable future.
8. I am reluctant to taking risks unless unavoidable.
9. Appearance is important to me.
10. I do not dispose of things that are usable.

Mike determined that he had a survival need level of about two-plus on the scale. Since he had been in the Marines, he had learned to take care of himself and could count on his training to keep himself safe in most situations. He was a skilled construction worker and believed that he could always support himself and his family. His children were important to him and they were a key element in his decision to be close to average in survival.

The primary survival need that was not being met in Mike's case was the survival of the species. Mike stated that he has always been protective of his daughter. This is not uncommon with the men of my groups. He felt powerless to control the safety of his daughter while he was out of a loving relationship with her. Mike viewed the other man as a threat to his child and judged Judy as putting his child in a dangerous situation. He thought that the medication on the table where his daughter could get to it was a hazard and he wanted to keep his daughter safe from such hazards.

Love and Belonging

The need for love and belonging drives our social behavior. It feels good to us to be connected with others, to be understood and to be thought of by others. The elements of love and belonging are friendship, caring, and involvement. Involvement with others brings us happiness. For a toddler, the love and belonging need is primarily met by the immediate family and a few close family friends. In the teens, people rely more on their own friends and when they get married and go out on their own, they have a mate and their own family primarily to meet this need.

The following ten statements helped Mike determine his level of love and belonging.

1. Love and intimacy are important to me.
2. I care for other people's welfare.
3. I am willing to spare my time for others.
4. I talk to the person next to me while traveling.
5. I like being with other people.
6. I maintain friendly relationships with acquaintances.
7. My spouse should have a deep concern about me.
8. I want other people to like me.
9. I am kind to other people.
10. I want my spouse to be fond of everything that is related to me.

Mike perceived that his relationship with Judy was bad and not satisfying his needs. He thought that he had a need level of four because he wanted to have people in his life that he loved. He had not been meeting this need because he had been pushing his loved ones away with his anger. Mike had been married before and his total behavior of angering and raging had made him undesirable to his wife. They had divorced and she had custody of his son. Instead of changing, Mike just went out and created another family with Judy. Mike perceived that Judy was preventing him from having a good relationship with his daughter. Mike was blaming Judy for this distancing just as he blamed his ex-wife for his lack of relationship with his son.

Blaming others for their problems is typical of people who have not learned Choice Theory or to take responsibility for their actions. Since they think they can control others, they think others can control them, too—the world is an external control model. They do not understand that being *attractive* is more successful in a relationship than being controlling. Mike's total behavior was making him less attractive to Judy and his daughter. It actually frightened them away from him. He would have to change his behavioral system and total behavior before he could attract Judy and his daughter back into his life.

Power

The need for power, achievement, and self-worth drives our productive behavior. Positive self-worth is tied to the basic need for power and is derived from accomplishing quality work. When we are effective, we feel proud and worthwhile; when we are not successful, we feel frustrated and our self-worth suffers. The elements of power are competence, achievement, recognition, importance, skill, and respect. The power needs are more internal than external.

Many, but not all, group members are laborers or unemployed with, at most, a high school diploma. Their self-esteem is low and they do not think they are highly respected in the community. They often come to group saying that their partner *disrespected* them and that is why they tried to force her to respect them. By "disrespected" they mean that the person did not ask for permission to do or say something (as though they had authority over that person to give permission). Reaching a point in your life where you feel that you are competent at something and have achieved a certain level of recognition and importance is an internal concept. The competence comes from within oneself and not by recognition from the community. Many people have gained community recognition without feeling the elements of power in their lives. These people continue to strive for more and more power and control over others.

Often there is a delicate balance between power and love and belonging because, unless treated properly, the two are at cross purposes with each other. Power can be an individual goal requiring individual control over the surrounding environment and people, whereas love and belonging is a mutual commitment and often requires give and take and equality of importance between individuals. Those in powerful positions have to be very careful of their family commitments to maintain the balance of love and belonging in their relationships. Power over oneself and one's choices can appear as aloofness, pushing people away from relationships. It is this internal power that satisfies our power needs instead of power over other people.

The following ten statements helped Mike determine his level of power.

1. I want to be recognized by my job by others.
2. I advise other people.
3. I give direction to other people.
4. I want to become well off compared to other people.
5. I like to be praised by others.
6. I do not hesitate when firing my staff.
7. I want to be outstanding in my field.
8. I want to be a leader in any group.
9. I consider myself as a valuable person.
10. I am proud of my accomplishments and talent.

Mike stated that he felt powerless to control a given situation, so he used his physical power in an attempt to satisfy his power need. He thought that his power need was at a level of three-plus, but conceded that it may be more important than his love and belonging need, which he had described as level four. This shows the difficulty he had in trying to separate these two needs to arrive at an evaluation of each, independent of the other. After a discussion of the issue, he still thought that his power need was less than his love and belonging need. Since there is no absolute test for the level of these needs, these levels are still self-report statistics.

The more he tried to hold on to his relationship with Judy and his daughter, the more they slipped away from him. It is like trying to hold onto a handful of dry sand—the harder you squeeze the more sand you lose. Mike wanted to control the situation and force his solution on the others so he exerted external control over Judy and the other man. His solution was basic. He wanted Judy to be a stay-at-home wife. In that manner, Mike could satisfy his need for power and control over Judy and his daughter. Mike was replaying a scenario that resulted in trouble with his ex-wife and son.

Freedom

The need for freedom drives us to be independent and to choose our own course. When we try to determine the behavior and choices of others, they do not like it. It inhibits their basic need for freedom. The elements of freedom are choice, autonomy, independence, and liberty. Freedom is a coveted concept. Being able to choose what satisfies our needs instead of being subjected to the choices that satisfy others' needs is the basis for happiness. There is a delicate balance between freedom and love and belonging because it demands opposite characteristics in a relationship. Autonomy and independence imply that others are not consulted in the decision-making process. Love and belonging, on the other hand, implies that others are taken into consideration when making a decision because it affects those who are close to you. With freedom, others are considered, but just not consulted as to their wishes and desires. People do not like our actions and shy away from us when we try to determine their total behavior and choices. It inhibits their basic need for freedom. Therein lays the major cause of conflict in all relationships.

The following ten statements helped Mike determine his level of freedom.

1. I don't like other people telling me what to do.
2. I can't stand being forced to do things that I don't like to do.
3. I believe that I shouldn't tell other people how to live.
4. I believe everybody has a right to live in his or her own way.
5. I believe that human beings have ability to make a free choice.
6. I want to do things that I want and when I want.
7. I want to live my way regardless of what other people say.
8. I believe every human being is born free.
9. I don't want to interfere with my spouse's freedom.
10. I believe I am open-minded.

Mike did not consider his need for freedom when he chose to act out his perceptions with total behavior that included threatening acts. He stated that his freedom need was below average and thought it to be about two or two-plus. Mike's love and belonging need was definitely higher than his freedom need because he placed his need for his daughter and Judy above his need to be without them. But, he admitted that he was thinking only of himself and not in the long term when he entered the apartment.

Mike did not consider the possibility that the legal system might take away his freedom for a period of time by putting him in jail. He did not consider that he might be on probation for up to three years, giving the court control over him for that period of time. He also did not consider that Judy would choose not to be around him or have their daughter around him because of his angering. Thinking is a component of total behavior. Mike did not think of the consequences of his actions prior to acting out with a violent action.

Fun

The need for fun drives our search for discovery and our interest in play. The elements of fun are pleasure, enjoyment, liberty, and learning. You will notice that liberty is both a part of freedom and of fun. Liberty brings fun into a life, as opposed to constraint, which brings tension and frustration into life. Fun includes going to Disneyland or the park for a family picnic. Fun is enjoying what you are doing. Learning can also be considered as fun. Remember when you were five or six years old and you learned a new song or joke or how to play with a yo-yo or a new computer game? It was fun and you wanted to share that fun with those around you, especially your family and close friends. Love and belonging, too, is a part of the fun need and that is why love and belonging is the key element in happiness.

The following ten statements helped Mike determine his level of fun.

1. I like laughing aloud.
2. I like jokes and humorous stories.
3. Sometimes I laugh at myself.
4. I am willing to learn new and useful things.
5. I like playing interesting games.
6. I like traveling around.
7. I like reading books.
8. I like going to the movies.

9. I like listening to the music.
10. I like creative ways of working and thinking.

Mike was unable to connect with any of his fun needs that were affected by the incident. He thought that his fun need was about average, a three on the scale. He did admit that being in the group was a learning experience and stated that he enjoyed coming to the sessions each week. It provided a place for him to get his head on straight and discuss his week's events. He also enjoyed helping other clients with their issues. After a discussion, Mike decided that he had sacrificed some of his fun needs by being in jail and controlled by the judge.

He did not see any fun in what happened in the incident that brought him to the group. This indicates that his chosen total behavior did not satisfy all of his needs. He did not choose a total behavior that addressed his fun need. This is typical of abusive aggressive behavior. There is often little or no fun in it for you or those you hold close to you. Aggressive acts encompass most, if not all, of the deadly habits. Aggressive acts push people away instead of bringing them closer to us and aggression violates the ultimate question. They are not fun.

The overall rating of Mike's generic needs is Survival, two-plus; Love and Belonging, four; Power, three-plus; Freedom, two or two-plus; and Fun, three. This rating describes a fairly average person.

Quality World

The quality world is the source of all important behavior. It contains what we want most. As we go through life, we build a special place in our memory that is filled with specific ways to satisfy one or more of our basic needs. The quality world is the most important part of our lives. We feel very good when the elements in our quality world are satisfied. It feels very bad and we are frustrated when the elements are not satisfied. Our quality world consists of people, situations, and beliefs that satisfy our five basic needs. The quality world is personal, not external or worldly. No two individual's quality worlds are the same.

For a couple to have a long-time, loving relationship, Dr. Glasser and Carleen Glasser (2000) state that their quality worlds must be similar. Most likely, they will differ only in the intensity of quality of the elements within the world. We pay attention, will work hard for what is in our quality world, and do not care much for what is not closely related to elements within it. The elements in our quality world usually take the form of pictures, ideas, or concepts that we believe will satisfy one or more of our needs. We store the memory of experiences that, at the time of occurrence, felt good and satisfied one or more of our generic needs.

Our quality world is built from the way we picture and perceive three very common but different kinds of life experiences: interactions with important people; interactions with things; and systems of belief that drive the total behavior from the behavioral system. The pictures in our quality world are very important and difficult to change because they were built on good feelings. Our choices are governed by our wanting to feel as good as we can now and in the future. In our quality world, we hold pictures of people, things, and beliefs that we have enjoyed in the past, are enjoying now, or hope to enjoy in the future. These pictures stay in our quality world until replaced by something that brings us more joy. This is the reason that we have such a great difficulty dealing with divorce and death. Both of these events alter our quality world with sadness instead of joy. The main criteria for keeping a picture in our quality world is how good the feeling or experience was when we chose to put it in. This is one of the reasons that people stay in intimate relationships—the initial love relationship is such a good experience that it is very difficult to remove it and the person from our quality world. We spend our time desperately trying to recapture the pleasure we had when we courted each other. This initial love relationship often masks the violence in an angering home and sets the victim up to remain in the relationship and continue being abused. Many of the pictures we hold in our quality world come from stories of how people should behave, such as fairy tales, movies, TV, and other storybook experiences. We picture how a wife should behave and love us. Our children are often princes or princesses. The key word in these pictures is *should*, because when these people do not live up to our pictures, we are disappointed and frustrated and anger over the differences. When we try to hold the people with whom we have relationships to these unrealistic pictures, we are often disappointed and chose anger as a means to express our disappointment.

For example, Mike had friends in his quality world that Judy did not even know. I, for one, was such a person. Judy knew about me and my relationship with Mike, but she had never met me or communicated with me in any manner. There are elements in our quality world that are not secret from our loved ones, but are still held to be very important. This just shows that, even for those closest to us, we do not know how important the elements in their quality world are to them. Respecting these unknown parts of our loved ones places the relationship above our self interest. In other words, the relationship is greater than each of us who are in the relationship.

Mike had Judy and his daughter in his quality world. Mike also had his son by his ex-wife in his quality world, even though he was not able to visit him as often as he would have liked. Mike also had the belief that he could overpower others to get them to do as he wished. He had been able to use force to get what he wanted, and so he believed that if he wanted something, it must be right for him to have it. If Mike ruled the world, he would have everybody do as he wanted and be the way he wanted them to be.

Mike also believed that it was wrong to snitch on Judy in order to have the authorities intervene. He could simply tell Judy how to run her life. He knew that he could not control the authorities and did not trust them to do things as he would do them. He could tell Judy how to take care of their daughter and she should do as he said. He did not consider her need for freedom. He had little or no empathy for Judy, or for his daughter, either. He could not put himself in Judy's shoes and accept her for who she was and what she had in her quality world. Remember, a home that looked neat and orderly was not in Judy's quality world. Judy's quality world picture was not a home that resembled a barracks.

Perceptual System

The perception system consists of the physical sensory system, the total knowledge that we have accumulated over the years of our lives, and the values we place on what we perceive. It is how we perceive the real world. The only way we know the real world exists is through our ability to perceive it through our senses. All of our senses make up the sensory system.

Sensory System

This system includes touch, sight, hearing, smells, and tastes. We develop likes and dislikes on each of the things that we sense. We relate to the real world by use of our sensory system. Everything that we sense is evaluated by our senses as it is transferred from the real world into our perceived world. For example, if you wear glasses, as I do, then the lenses alter the real-world image in such a manner as to correct for the distortion in our sight system. The smells that we bring in through our noses are compared with the learning of smells that we experienced when we were children. The smell of mother's apple pie cooling in the kitchen or chicken frying in the pan is an example of these smells. The principle applies to our sense of taste. Our hearing sensitivity is subject to any birth defects or abuse we may have encountered in our life. Our touch sensitivity and detection system is honed to a fine point by use and observation of the items that we encounter. We start developing our knowledge of senses when we are born and continue through out our lives.

Total Knowledge Filter

Our total knowledge filter contains all of the facts and concepts understood or experienced. It does not place any value, positive or negative, on the knowledge. This filter separates the perceptions into three categories— rejection as meaningless, acceptance conditionally until we can find out if it is meaningful or not, and acceptance absolutely because it is meaningful to us. The total knowledge filter rejects those things that we know to be unimportant or irrelevant to our current situation. We totally disregard those elements of the real world that we deem to be irrelevant and not connected with our thoughts and ideas. The filter lets those things that we think might be pertinent to the subject we are addressing and concerned with to pass to the valuing filter. The perceptions that are passed through the total knowledge filter are then evaluated by the valuing filter.

Valuing Filter

The valuing filter is the one we use to place value on those elements and thoughts that pass through our sensory system and total knowledge filter. These are the elements that are meaningful or the ones we want to find out about. We compare each element of the current situation with our values and quality world pictures, and then place a level of pain or joy to each. This level can go from very painful for unsatisfying feelings or negative values, through neutral values when we have no feelings about an element, to very pleasurable for satisfying feelings or positive values. We tend to put a negative value or pain on what we perceive if it opposes anything we want. We tend to put a positive value or pleasure on what we perceive if it matches our quality world. We tend to put a neutral value on what we perceive if it is neither opposed to, nor particularly close to, anything we want.

The sensory system and total knowledge filter directly relate to our survival need in that pungent odors protect us, dangerous sights and sounds warn us, and unpleasant touches separate us from dangers.

Enticing smells or tastes, on the other hand, can encourage us to eat too much and endanger our physical health. Therefore, we must apply our valuing filter to that which the sensory system senses by using the total knowledge that we have learned. Our basic needs are interconnected, not individual and distinct needs.

Mike perceived the external control of the judge as unfair, and thought that his own actions were justified. Mike kept saying, "I only wanted to talk with the man." Mike did not think about how he looked to Judy or the other man. Our actions communicate twice as much information as the words that we speak. Unless we are looking in a mirror, we are unlikely to know really how we look to others. Dancers and actors practice in front of a mirror so that they will know how it feels to look a certain way to the audience.

Mike perceived the pills on the table as a threat to the safety of his daughter. He perceived the messy home as *dirty* and not as a fit place to raise a child. He perceived Judy as the person who was responsible for all of this danger to his daughter. He perceived the other man as the threat to his continued life with Judy and his daughter. Mike had a prior marriage and another child. The prior wife would not let him see that child after their separation. He perceived that there was no one who could help him so he needed to take matters into his own hands.

Perceived World

Our perceived world consists of our perceptions along with the values we place on them. It contains many more pictures and concepts than our quality world. It contains the total history of the perceptions that we have gained during our lives. Our perceived world represents our total knowledge, or what we can remember of it. We take this world and compare it with our quality world. It is from our perceived world that we generate the frustrations from painful feelings, the pleasures from happy feelings, and the acceptance from those feelings that do not have a bearing on the present situation. This is the way we see the world. It is very dependent upon our historical upbringing, current self-esteem, and the self-worth we feel and our ability to deal with the situation at hand. No two perceived worlds are the same because each of us has different experiences. What we perceive as reality or the real world is, therefore, not real or objective, but subjective to our background. The reason that we can get along with each other is that many of us perceive the world in similar ways.

When you talk with people about the actions of your pet dog or cat, you are visualizing your pet, but they are visualizing their own unless they know yours and have its image in their minds. We must remember that this same visualization occurs when we are talking with anyone about either our issues or theirs. Our perceptions are not the same as any other person's, and we must allow for that difference in making decisions regarding our perceptions.

Realities, objectivity, sanity, truth, right, wrong, good, and bad are a few examples of what we believe as real. The reality of aggression in an argument is also a matter of perception. If the more aggressive person believes that he was too aggressive, he might minimize his actions to render these actions more acceptable to society. The group members help each other learn that others might not view the world in the same manner. This is a vital part of the group process and dynamics.

If Mike snitched on Judy for the dirty house, he thought that Child Protective Services would take his daughter away from him, put her up for adoption, and he would be unable to see her again. He perceived a world without his daughter and Judy as very painful. Mike's perceived world did not match his quality world. Mike believed that he has always had a good, caring, and non-violent relationship with his daughter.

Comparing Place

The comparing place is where the real world, as perceived by the person and evaluated in the perceived world, is compared with the quality world.

We receive information through our senses and combine that information with what we already know into a perception, a picture of our current reality. We are constantly comparing what we perceive with what we want. If there is a match, we may ignore the situation or we may continue to act the way we are already acting. If there is not a match, we try to decide how to change our total behavior so as to bring the two into equilibrium. When they are in equilibrium, we are happy and at peace with our lives.

Differences are evaluated to determine if a total behavior action has to be taken in an attempt to bring the perceived world and the quality world into equilibrium. Our total behavior is our best attempt at the time to act upon, or deal with, the real world so we can best satisfy our needs and the pictures from our quality world that address those needs. We become aware that our quality world picture is not the same as the perceptions that we have of the real world, so we try to bring the two into balance. When there is little or no commonality between our perceived world and our quality world, we experience a brief involuntary total behavior that is usually painful. We then go on to create a new organized behavior to correct the situation and bring the two back into balance. This total behavior will always be our best attempt at the time to try to take more effective control of the situation. We may find out shortly after making the attempt that it was not effective and, in fact, may have made the situation worse or more out of balance. This is often the case when people use violence and force to gain control of others. These efforts may or may not be effective, but they all represent attempts to restore a sense of inner balance and control over the situation.

If we compare this personal behavior control system to that of the visual control system of driving a car, we will conclude that it is very soft, or not a very direct control system. When driving a car on dry pavement around a corner, we turn the wheel as much as we have learned to turn it from past experiences. If we see that we need to make a correction and turn the wheel either less or more, we do so, and the car takes an equivalent change in the turning rate unless we are traveling too fast and start to skid. The friction between the tires and the road is sufficient to allow us to have a direct or tight control over the turning rate of the car. If we are driving on ice, however, the car may not turn at the rate we want and we may even lose control of the car. The friction between the tires and the ice does not allow us to have a direct control over the turning rate due to the speed at which we are traveling. The personal behavior control system is much like the car being driven on ice. We do not have direct control of the real world's reaction to our total behavior. In fact, we have no control over others. We have to choose our behavior very carefully, considering the ultimate question to maintain the greatest control over our personal happiness in order to steer our way through the maze of life's experiences and our relationships with others.

Mike was afraid to use Child Protective Services (CPS) to assist in getting the home cleaned up and safe for his daughter. He thought that if CPS came to the home and saw it the way he perceived it, they would take his daughter away from Judy. He thought that they would put his daughter in a foster home, because he had the prior domestic violence conviction and would not be judged fit to take care of his daughter. When I explained the operation of CPS to Mike, the additional information allowed him to come to a different belief and solution to his problem. He called CPS and asked them to make an assessment of Judy's apartment and living conditions. When the social worker perceived the apartment, the social worker asked Judy to clean it up to a point that provided safety for their daughter, but was below Mike's expectations. Judy complied and CPS was satisfied and closed the case. Mike was relieved that his child had not been taken away from Judy and satisfied by the outside evaluation of the apartment.

Mike thought that if the other man came into Judy's life, he would take Mike's place in his daughter's life, too. He thought that he would lose her to this man just as he lost his son from the previous relationship.

Mike thought that he was between a rock and a hard place. He could not figure any other way to take control of the situation. His behavioral system suggested Mike had to take over and make things right. He could not think of any other things to do to take more effective control of the situation. He had to take care of things the only way his behavioral system could suggest. Mike had to step in and make things right.

Behavioral System

Our behavioral system has the capability of storing and organizing previous behaviors. The system categorizes them as to their ability to balance the comparing place. It can also create new total behaviors to bring effective control into our lives. When our worlds are in balance and we are in effective control of our lives, we tend to pay little attention to what we are continually creating in the way of total behaviors. We are on automatic control. When we encounter a situation in which our automatic control has not balanced our perceived world with our quality world, we then develop more creative total behaviors. We become desperate for something more effective than what we have been using. Our creative behaviors may not seem effective to others, but they are the best that we can generate at the time. Sometimes our creative behaviors seem self-destructive or painful to others, especially when force and aggression are used. Aggression has the end result of distancing others from us and not satisfying our love and belonging need. Remember, the best total behavior is one that helps to satisfy all five of the needs, not one need at the cost of another.

Not only is the expression of anger learned, but it can become a routine, familiar, and predictable response to a variety of situations. When angering is displayed frequently and aggressively, it can become a maladaptive habit because it results in negative consequences. Habits, by definition, are performed over and over again, without thinking. People with angering problems often resort to aggressive displays of anger to solve their problems, without thinking about the negative consequences they may suffer or the debilitating effects it may have on the people around them.

Much of our group work is creating behaviors that will help us to gain effective control of our lives while not attempting to control others. The first of the ten axioms, "The only person whose behavior we can control is our own," is discussed many times in the group. It is one of the hardest axioms to be accepted completely. Another element of Choice Theory that is often referred to in the group is the ultimate question—

If I do or say (fill in the blank), will it bring us closer together (caring habits) or will it push us farther apart (deadly habits)?

The habits are given by Dr. Glasser in many of his books:

- Seven Deadly Habits
  - Criticizing
  - Blaming
  - Complaining
  - Nagging
  - Threatening
  - Punishing
  - Rewarding to control

- Seven Caring Habits
  - Supporting
  - Encouraging
  - Listening
  - Accepting
  - Trusting
  - Respecting
  - Negotiating differences

Mike's prior behavior taught him that he could overpower others to get what he wanted. He had been raised in a tough neighborhood where he got his way by overpowering others. Mike had been a Marine in Viet Nam and had learned that *might makes right,* so, if you wanted something, all you had to do was take it. He did not stop to think about the response that the real world might have to his total behavior. Nor did he stop to consider his caring feelings for Judy and his daughter. Had he done so, Mike might have slowed his aggressive advance and used some of the caring habits such as listening, trusting, and respecting. Instead, Mike used the deadly habits of complaining, blaming, criticizing, and threatening. He let his feelings of powerlessness dictate his total behavior.

I pointed out to Mike that the difference between criticism and feedback is that criticism places a value judgment on the situation or event and feedback just reports what happened or what was left out. There is no criticism in pure feedback.

When Mike used the CPS to evaluate Judy's apartment living conditions, he used a new set of total behaviors in his behavioral system. This is the learning that goes on while the clients are members of the group. Mike also learned that if he became more attractive in his behavior, then Judy would not be repelled by his actions and would, instead, want Mike in her and their daughter's lives.

Total Behavior

Total behavior consists of four inseparable components. They are *thinking, acting, feeling,* and *physiology.* Similar to the picture of the car in Chapter Four, the front two wheels steer the car; the thinking and acting are the ones that we can consciously control. The rear wheels represent the last two—feeling and physiology—and they are created as a result of the body's reaction to the incident, what you think about it, and the actions that you take as a result from the behavioral system. Many therapists think these are the driving force behind the actions we take, but Choice Theory teaches us *we have cognitive control of the body forces and can determine our best plan of actions.* That is, we can steer the car by the front wheels and control the force on the gas pedal, but we cannot steer the car by the rear wheels. As we give up our controlling behaviors, false pride, over-competitiveness, and striving for power, we become more accessible to family and friends. We become more attractive in relationships.

We identify the behavior by the strongest signal. There is a definite thought, action, and body sensation that happens at the same time as the feeling. When we say we are frustrated, the feeling of frustration is the strongest signal. The same is true for angry, happy, in love, etc.

Powerlessness is experienced by an individual when things do not go as desired. This feeling generates frustration. The aggressor becomes frustrated over current events, frustrated over surrounding conditions, frustrated over not being able to accomplish desired tasks, or frustrated with other people's actions/behaviors.

Powerlessness is the underlying feeling in the generation of anger within the physical body. All of the other feelings of anger stem from the original sense that you cannot be more powerful than some event, concept, or person. Something or someone else appears to be controlling you or what is happening to you. The aggressor thinks that he is the victim of external control. Remember, it is not the external control that makes you angry. It is how you choose to totally behave regarding the powerlessness that you feel that leads to your choice to anger.

Power gives a perception of being in control and it is heightened by an increased energy level. Therefore, power and anger can have the same feeling. The more successful the use of anger is to control others, the more it is used even if it is destructive to the life of the user. As a young person, anger worked to get your parents to satisfy your needs—the crying of a baby brings food, clean diapers, and gets them picked up and held, etc. If you are allowed to use anger to get your needs satisfied when you grow up, you never learn how to negotiate your needs and to solve problems for yourself. Some call this maturing, and if so, then the clients are asked to mature in the group so that they can get their needs met without the use of aggression.

Anger is often expressed as:

- Non-support, silence, sabotage,
- Tone of voice, volume of voice,
- Throwing items in the presence of spouse,
- Throwing items at spouse,

- Throwing the spouse herself,
- Hitting walls, tables and other items as though they were the spouse,
- Hitting spouse or children.

Powerlessness is a necessary feeling for the expression of anger and is always present when a person feels and expresses anger. The feeling of powerlessness has not been determined to be sufficient, in and of itself, to cause anger or a violent expression of anger. Other factors of total behavior must be present to generate the violent expression of anger. The manner in which angering is expressed is dependent upon many factors and their presence, or absence, at the moment of feeling powerless. The thought of being less than sufficient to control a situation is often present when the feeling of powerlessness occurs.

Some of these factors and their relationship to the expression of anger are well known. Others are subtle and do not always contribute to violence with anger. Alcohol is one of the most prevalent factors in the acting out of anger in a violent manner toward another person. It reduces self-control and allows a violent person to act out their anger in violent ways. Additional preconditions may be present which add to the expression of violent anger. These include the following beliefs in a behavioral system:

- It is OK to use violence to get your way.
- There is a king of the castle.
- The man is the boss.
- I am right!

The behavioral system contains over-learned behaviors, i.e., behaviors that have been used successfully for many years. Over-learned behaviors are very difficult to manage. Anger is an over-learned behavior. Getting angry and acting out works from childhood to adult life. The success of anger and violence is learned and utilized until it becomes second nature. People lie to themselves to justify the anger. The person believes the lies are true and uses them to justify the violence. Anger wears many masks:

- The mask of stress and anxiety,
- The mask of entitlement,
- The mask of control,
- The mask of fantasy,
- The mask of shame,
- The mask of embarrassment.

There are physiological (physical) warning signs, acting (behavioral) warning signs and thinking (cognitive), or feeling (emotional) warning signs. The physiological warning signs include increased blood pressure, tension, increased heart rate, sweating, shaking, and dizziness. The acting warning signs include throwing things, hitting things or people, and yelling. The thinking warning signs include finding yourself thinking thoughts of blame against the other person, thinking that you are justified in taking the stance that you are taking, or thinking that you have no control over the situation. The feeling warning signs are those of helplessness, powerlessness, bitterness, anger, and resentment.

Mike described his total behavior as follows:

Physiology—Mike was tense, agitated, and had an elevated heart rate, i.e., physiology of anger.
Acting—When operating on autopilot, Mike's behavioral system had him act out his total behavior in violence and an aggressive act.
Feeling—Mike had feelings of frustration, desperation, terror, loneliness, and unhappiness.
Thinking—Mike thought he was powerless to change things; he had terrifying thoughts of danger to his daughter and of losing Judy; and he felt that he had to take things into his own hands and fix them.

Mike admitted in group that he did not use the thinking component as frequently as he could and stated he would like to make a change in his behavioral system, i.e., think before you act. In particular, he wanted to be able to think about what the reaction of the real world could be if he took a particular action. If the reaction of the real world would be contrary to the desired outcome, then he would try to think of a different total behavior or ask others for guidance and suggestions.

Real World

The existence of the real world is known, but it cannot be perceived accurately. We use the real world to satisfy our basic needs, but only through our own perceptions. The real world consists of facts, concepts, and items. We can assess the effect of the facts on our lives, but the concepts are cognitive in nature and the understanding of them is modified by our perceptions. Similarly, the essentials of the real world can only be perceived through our senses—touch, smell, taste, sound, and sight. The actions of the real world in response to our total behavior can be evaluated and labeled.

In Mike's case, the real world reacted in a way that he thought was harsh. The real world, as represented by law enforcement and judicial systems and Judy, reacted to his total behavior by arresting him for vandalism because of the broken bedroom door, placing him in jail for thirty days, and fining him $350 plus court costs. The court also required him to perform twenty days of community service, and to attend fifty-two weeks of domestic violence classes of two hours each week. In addition, Judy did not want to have Mike around her or their daughter when he was acting in a violent manner, so she obtained a restraining order against Mike. The court did give Mike monitored visitation with his daughter, but Judy could not be the monitor and she had to approve of the monitor that Mike chose.

The court wanted Mike to become a non-violent person who would not react to his frustrations with violence. Mike chose my group, which happened to include instruction in Choice Theory, to satisfy the punishment that the court issued. This allowed Mike to take a different approach in his life's decisions and attitudes. This additional information is what he used to make a self-assessment of his behavioral system and to consider making some changes in it.

We have considered all of the elements of the flow chart and Mike's reaction to them. The information that Mike gave and got during his self-evaluation helped both him and the other members of the group because many of them had been thinking and acting in a similar manner. That is one of advantages of a group over individual counseling. An additional advantage is that the members of the group input information to each other, in addition to that which the group facilitator can provide.

I told Mike, "It all goes back to what I said earlier. You can always change your perceptions, or what you want, or your behavior. The actions of others create moments for you to make your choices. No one controls your response to his or her actions. You are the one who makes your choices to satisfy your needs. It all comes down to what you want and your ability to make non-violent choices."

I continued, "Once you accept the fact that you are always in control of what you perceive, what you want, and what you do, you have a huge responsibility. You are accountable for the meaning you place on the information you receive. You are also accountable for what you want and the total behaviors you choose to get what you want. Just remember that you are always making choices, whether you do it consciously or unconsciously. You are in control of you."

Mike was given the homework assignment of completing a chart (Wubbolding, 2000) of his wants, behavior, assessment, and plan for improving his relationship with Judy and his daughter. Happiness is the end result of Mike's decision to change his total behavior and worldview.

MIKE'S SELF EVALUATION CHART

CHOICE THEORY IDEAS	QUESTIONS YOU CAN ASK YOURSELF	FILL IN YOUR ANSWERS HERE, KEEPING CHOICE THEORY IN MIND
BASIC NEEDS • Survival • Belonging • Power • Freedom • Fun **QUALITY WORLD:** Specific pictures of people, things, systems of belief linked to the needs	• What do I need in this situation? • What specifically do I want that I am not getting? • What do I see in my real world that is not matching my quality world pictures? • What is my ideal picture?	**Wants:** Mike wanted relationships with Judy and his daughter that would satisfy his need for love and belonging. Mike did not feel that he was getting this need met and was afraid that he would be put out of their lives by this other man. He saw this other man taking his place with Judy and his daughter. His ideal picture has all three of them together and happy.

TOTAL BEHAVIOR
Acting   \ I can
Thinking / control
 	
Feeling   \ Indirectly
                  \ controlled
Physiology / by what I
                  / choose to do
	• Which component of my total behavior have I been focusing on to get what I want?
	• What choices am I making to get my needs met?
	• In my relationships with others, what am I choosing to do? Are we moving closer or farther apart?
	• Am I using any of the seven deadly habits?
		Behavior: Mike was focusing on his feelings of separation and used anger to force his solution on everyone.
		Mike was choosing his old behavior patterns of external control to get his way. They were moving him away from Judy and his daughter.
		He was using threats to try to get his way with Judy and his daughter.

MIKE'S SELF EVALUATION CHART Continued

CHOICE THEORY IDEAS	QUESTIONS YOU CAN ASK YOURSELF	FILL IN YOUR ANSWERS HERE, KEEPING CHOICE THEORY IN MIND
MY ASSESSMENT of the choices I have been making	• Whose behavior can I control? • Is my behavior working for me? If not … • Is what I am doing now going to get me more or less of what I want? • Am I using external control in my relationships? • Am I happy or unhappy with my current relationship?	**Assessment:** Through this self-evaluation process, Mike realized that his total behavior was counter-productive and that he can control only himself. He realized that his behavior was actually moving him farther away from his quality world and that the use of external control was making him unhappy in his current relationship.
TRUSTING MY CREATIVITY I can make a plan to be more effective.	• What can I do today that will improve my relationships? • If what I am choosing to do to get what I want is not working, what else could I do that might be more effective? • What is my plan? • Can my plan be started today and is it dependent only on my own behavior?	**Plan:** Mike decided to try using the caring habits and to stop trying to force the situation. He made a plan to use Choice Theory in his behavior and let Judy see that he had changed. He thought that this would attract her instead of forcing her to be in a relationship with him.

CHAPTER 9

Group Solution

The group assists in supporting and providing the caring habits to its members. The real world's reaction to his total behavior was sufficiently drastic to teach Mike that his choice of behaviors was unacceptable. A better choice for Mike would have been one where he could maintain his freedom while still satisfying his survival and love and belonging needs. Mike was able to evaluate his behavior and determine where he could have made better choices by discussing each of the elements of the chart. The elements of his quality world (*snitching*), the importance of his freedom need, and how Child Protective Services could assist in getting his love and belonging and survivability needs met were evaluated. Mike was also able to realize how his past training and parenting had established a behavioral system that did not serve him well in times of crisis. Mike learned that his total behavior could be non-productive when he did not think about the reaction that the real world might have if he became violent. The discussion in class gave Mike the information that Child Protective Services seldom takes children from parents for a dirty home unless the parents cannot get the home cleaned up and safe for the children. Mike also learned that a change to using the seven caring habits could strengthen his relationship with Judy. The result of that change might lessen Judy's desire to be with other men. Mike would become more attractive to Judy. This would help to satisfy his love and belonging need.

Mike's Current Situation

Mike completed the homework assignment by answering the questions in the four areas: wants, behavior, assessment, and plan. Mike had three basic choices to consider. They are to leave the relationship either physically and or emotionally, to change the relationship by using the deadly habits to control Judy, or to negotiate a solution to the problem areas and accept the relationship as it is without the use of the deadly habits. His wants included having Judy and his daughter in his life. Mike wanted to be the only love of Judy, as well as the only father figure for his daughter. Mike realized he would have to earn these positions and that they would not just be granted to him. Mike realized that his past behavior system had failed him in his family situation. He would have to change some of the elements in his behavior system in order to turn his relationships around and realize his wants. Mike assessed his behavior and realized that his attitude was driving Judy and his daughter away. This was contrary to his wants, so Mike decided to use the caring habits instead of the deadly habits of external control to accomplish his goals of a happy family.

Mike and Judy decided to reunite. Mike cleans the apartment to his satisfaction and is accepting of Judy's lack of a need for tidiness. Mike continued in domestic violence groups and shared his Choice Theory successes. Mike concluded his fifty-two weeks in the group, but still struggles with the use of force and anger to solve his problems. He has not acted out with violence since initially joining the group. Mike supported others in finding better choices to their situations while he was in the group. These new choices satisfy their needs and wants instead of forcing their way on others.

Another example of how the group provides support to its members is demonstrated by the story of Paul. Paul participated in the group discussions about Choice Theory and was beginning to take responsibility for his actions by admitting that he had used external force to control his girlfriend. He had been violence-free since coming to the group. He was demonstrating an understanding of and practiced positive conflict resolution skills. Paul demonstrated an understanding that the use of coercion or violent behavior to maintain dominance is unacceptable in an intimate relationship. He had not made threats to harm anyone in any manner. This is just one of the many interventions that the group makes with its members in support of them making the difficult decisions to change their way of reacting to the events in their lives.

Paul's Story

Our group sessions are two hours long with a ten minute break. During one session, we were discussing an event where the police had been videotaped kicking and hitting a man with little apparent reason. The community was outraged over the situation and was waiting for the outcome of the three independent investigations that were being conducted. I had discussed the situation with some police officers and heard their perception of the situation. They also gave some suggestions of the things that could have occurred that might contribute to the credibility of the police's actions.

The discussion centered on the use of force and the choice of angering by the police officers. Several of the group members expressed the opinion that the police were allowed to use force and, yet, they were in the group because they used force. They did not think that it was just. We discussed the use of external control by the community and the role that they could play in changing their immediate community by teaching their families about Choice Theory and by using it themselves in their total behaviors.

After the break, Paul came back to the group late. He explained that he had just been told that his brother had been shot in New York and that he was in critical condition. I asked him how he was feeling and he responded that he was angry, afraid for his brother, and sad over the situation. This was his younger brother, the baby in the family, and Paul had been careful to make sure that he attended school and stayed away from the gangs in his neighborhood. Paul wanted his brother to grow up right and make something of himself. I asked Paul about the other elements of total behavior and he responded that he was tense and anxious and wanted to "get rid of the energy that he felt inside." He thought he wanted to go back to New York and take care of matters himself. He was sitting in his chair with his head hung low and looked as though he was about to cry.

The other members of the group joined in the discussion by showing him compassion and caring about him and his brother. They suggested alternate actions that he could take that might bring about better results than "taking care of those who shot his brother." They suggested that he call his mother to get the latest facts about his brother's condition before making any decisions. They suggested that he use local law enforcement to deal with the situation and that he provide them with any information that he might obtain which would help police catch the aggressors. They suggested that he pray and stated that they would pray for his brother's recovery. One man suggested that he come over to his house for the night so that he could be with someone who cared and understood what he was going through. This man had had a similar experience with a good friend. The group supported Paul and by the end of the session, they had discouraged him from taking revenge and using violence to settle his feelings of powerlessness and anger. They encouraged him not to use external control to correct this perceived wrong.

As the time came for the group to end, the only comment that I could make was that I was very proud of the way they had come to Paul's aid, using Choice Theory to do so. These men were practicing what we had been learning in the previous sessions. Choice Theory works with aggressors, not only in a family situation, but also in a community, state, national, and worldly situation, too. They can learn it and use it in their everyday lives instead of resorting to violence and external control.

CHAPTER 10

Conclusion

We satisfy the five basic needs through the ideal world, which we create in our minds by storing memories of the pleasurable experiences we encounter and the dreams of the experiences we have. This ideal world is called the *quality world*. When we perceive that our *total behavior* meets our basic needs, the result is happiness and mental health. When our basic needs are not met, we feel unhappiness, which results in frustration, anger, and violence.

We are responsible for everything we do—no one else, just us! Reality Therapy with Choice Theory states that we choose all we do. The total behavior concept explains that we choose all behavior and that all behavior consists of four inseparable components: *acting, thinking, feeling*, and *physiology*. We can consciously choose the first two: how we act and what we think. We have indirect control over most of our feelings and some of our physiology by the choices we make about our thinking and acting. There is a large amount of creativity in almost every important total behavior that we choose. We choose all of our behavior and we are, therefore, responsible for all we choose.

The basic question that we work on in group is: "What can we control and change?" There are things that we can control and change—our perceptions, the things we want, and our behavior.

Unhappiness and angering results from the perception that we are powerless over persons, places, and things. We want to control them to our satisfaction. Angering starts with the frustration of not being able to make things the way we want them. As the frustration goes unsatisfied or denied, our anger increases. If we choose aggression as a component of our total behavior to deal with this frustration, it will be detrimental to our relationships and health. We tell ourselves lies to justify our aggression and to deny its effect on our lives. Angering leads to decreased problem solving, verbal and physical aggression, and often to a community reaction via the court system.

Judges use the fifty-two-week domestic violence program in cases of anger management or family aggression, when domestic partners are involved, even though there was no violence perpetrated on the partner. Judges also use mandated parenting classes to teach the parenting skills needed to raise healthy, well adjusted, and happy children. A man was sentenced to the group because he and his partner were caught engaging in rough sex. The neighbors and police thought that there was a fight going on in the apartment because of the noises that could be overheard. Another man proved in court that he did not touch or threaten his partner and that his partner was fabricating the incident. He was still sentenced to fifty-two weeks because the judge stated that when they argued verbally, they must have been disturbing the peace. One of the questions that arise is: "Is this appropriate application of the fifty-two-week program?" My answer is: Choice Theory and Reality Therapy are applicable to all individuals who have difficulty with angering in their relationships with others or with parenting their children. Exposure to Choice Theory certainly will not hurt anyone and it is each person's choice to use the principles or not.

My primary responsibility as a facilitator of domestic violence, family aggression, and parenting groups is to create a satisfying relationship with my clients. From this relationship, I can teach them to find increasingly healthier ways to relate to others in their lives. One of the questions that the facilitator is constantly considering is: "What is the effectiveness of the client's choices?" The client's reports of their choices in their relationships reveal the answer to this question. The facilitator is constantly teaching Choice Theory to the clients and helping them plan their future goals.

My experience as a facilitator of family aggression batterers groups for over a decade in Los Angeles probation-sanctioned programs and as a teacher in parenting groups has taught me that some personalities are extremely difficult or impossible to treat with a group program, even one based on Choice Theory. These people are a small proportion of the total of aggressors and they cannot be identified by the court system in advance. People who have been raised in cultures where male domination over women and children is the norm and who choose not to give up those beliefs in their quality world often learn that it is illegal to treat women and children in that fashion. Even knowing that it is illegal in this country, they do not surrender the belief and total behavior of forcing others to do their bidding. People who are too immature to give up the belief that they can control their world with force as the world controls them with force often repeat the aggressive behavior. Additionally, those with sociopathic or psychotic disorders have difficulty understanding and accepting the tenants of Choice Theory. The seventh axiom of Choice Theory states that all we can give or get from other people is information. How he deals with that information is the client's choice. This is true, but some clients have a difficult time adjusting to its reality.

As the client progresses through the fifty-two weeks, he is learning to evaluate the ultimate question before totally behaving with deadly habits.

Remember what John said: "I have to care about myself and act as though I do by using the caring habits with myself and not pushing myself away from myself before I can use the caring habits with anyone else." This is one of the basic keys to making lasting and meaningful changes in the client's behavioral system and total behavior.

An important part of our lives is simply tending to our basic needs—sitting down daily to share a meal with loved ones, getting enough sleep, setting time aside for haircuts and polishing shoes, and spending leisure time with friends. Paying attention to these things only when they become crises makes our lives unbalanced and crisis-oriented. Many men have neglected themselves because they felt it was the mark of a tough guy. Others have been so lost in an addiction or so codependent that respectful self-caring was not possible.

As we regain our sanity, we find balance in the basics. Self-love allows us to be responsible for our care, and it puts us in a stronger position to help others, to be creative, and to assert our right to recovery.

As Steve and Jill Morris state in *Leadership Simple: Leading People to Lead Themselves,* there are five questions that lead to recognizing and understanding our reality:

- What do you want?
- What are you doing to get what you want?
- Is it working to get what you want?
- What else can you do?
- What will you do?

These questions can come in many different forms, but they all deal with what can we control and change. Dr. Glasser and the Morrises call them Procedures That Lead to Change. The Morrises write to managers of company units, but their ideas can be used in a family as the parents are managers of the family unit. They state that managers recognize that the best way to lead people is to help others self-evaluate. Leadership is a conversation with and a journey between people. Choice Theory as applied to management is called Lead Management. It is a system that permits parents and children to navigate through the maze of each other's wants, perceptions, and behaviors.

When the five questions above are asked of a family, the members are led to think for themselves. They see how they can get what they want and how they can connect those wants with what the entire family needs. The counselor leads each family member to connect his or her map of reality with the maps of the other family members to create a map for the family as a whole. This family map is the family's road to peace, happiness, and a calm household.

Finally, as facilitator, I have to make an evaluation of the client's acceptance of the concept of Choice Theory by listening to him speak and to his statements about his total behavior. Additionally, I evaluate the client's commitment to live a life without violence as the first solution to his frustrating and angering. We are not just talking about a difference in the language that he uses, but in the examples that he gives regarding his dealings with others. The manner in which he thinks becomes apparent and is expressed in the words and the tone of voice he uses. The client demonstrates this language when talking about his partners, both former and present. I also have to make an assessment of the client's commitment to the concepts of living life with Choice Theory and without aggression. The second evaluation is with regard to the client's parenting concepts and skills. Choice Theory is a way of living, acting, and being in the family and society. It is not just a book-learned theory, but it is a way of life in total. Using Choice Theory eliminates the need for aggressive angering in the family. Choice Theory has proven to be an effective theory for use with persons who are aggressors within the family. It applies to the parenting skills exhibited by the parents. It can be extrapolated to all persons who have frustrating situations in their lives. It can also be extrapolated to our communities, states, nations, and to the entire world's population.

APPENDIX A

Exemplary Family, Lute and Terri

I have used the story of Lute and his wife, Terri, to illustrate the application of Reality Therapy with Choice Theory. The family consists of father, mother, and his/her/their children: his son by a different woman, her daughter by a different man and their daughter. This type of blended family is becoming more prevalent and our courts and communities have to deal with the anger and frustration that occurs as a result of failed relationships. This may appear to be a composite family, but in actuality, it is a genuine blended family. Lute attended my domestic violence groups while Terri attended my parenting classes and I monitored visits between the children and their fathers. This book addresses some of the problems that such a family may have and offers a means to overcome the ongoing relationship problems. The methods and information discussed within this book are used in domestic violence groups to satisfy court-ordered counseling and to assist the primary aggressor to learn to deal with the frustrations of life and in a relationship. They are also used in the parenting classes to help the parents bring about calmness between them and their children. Courts often do not require the entire family to attend counseling.

This example relates both Lute's and Terri's versions of their life together. Lute's version differs from Terri's version. The reader can see the manner in which Lute makes himself out to be a hero to the other members of a domestic violence group and Terri makes him out to be the villain and justifies her decision to stay away from him. Terri received counseling from her sheltered residence before moving back into the community and attended parenting classes after leaving the shelter. Each person's perception comes from the viewpoint of the person telling the story, and it may be different from what an unrelated third party may have experienced and reported. What real world version would a camera have reported?

Members of Lute's group give their unedited version of the events in their lives. With one-sided groups, the facilitator has to retain the perspective that the reports made by the group members are their perceptions and not necessarily, an accurate representation of what happened in real world. It is very difficult for an aggressive and controlling person to confess in front of fifteen other men that he beat or abused a woman. It is also difficult for parents to admit they do not know how to deal with a child or that what they learned from their parents is not correct. The offender knows what he or she did, but finds it difficult to admit it in public. Angering in the family in the form of aggressive acts against a mate and/or children takes place most often behind closed doors and is not discussed in public.

Often the reported versions change with time because the member becomes more at ease with the group and himself. When this occurs, the member may be more willing to acknowledge just how aggressive he was and what kind of physical and emotional abuse to which he may have subjected his partner or his children. Only then can true change occur in an aggressor's life.

Lute came to the domestic violence group and said, "I really want to make peace with my family. I want to stay out of the courts and jail. I saw my daughter walk for the first time and I want to see her grow up." He had been through considerable counseling and knew the language and concepts of psychology. He could talk the talk, but was not walking the walk.

I interpreted this to be a higher level of commitment—one that gives hope to the family and facilitator, although there can still be failure and reoccurrence of the aggression. This level does not commit Lute to 100 percent success, but it does restore the hope for a peaceful family in the future. The facilitator can report to the court that Lute has accepted the concepts of non-violent behavior and that he is reporting practice of them in his life. The judge was pleased to receive this report about Lute.

In group, Lute learned the language of Choice Theory and argues in favor of Choice Theory ideas and states examples of how he has utilized them in his relationships and at his job.

Terri reports a different picture of Lute. She says, "Lute is still doing drugs and I am afraid that he will get violent when things don't go his way—just the same way he did in the past. Lute still tries to control me by threatening to stop giving me money for our daughter if I stop seeing him."

Lute said. "When I saw my daughter walk for the first time, I made a decision to change my lifestyle and embrace a more peaceful and loving way of life."

Terri says, "Lute had seen his daughter walk before he was arrested, but he was doing drugs and, most likely, he didn't realize what he was seeing."

Lute has been a man of control and violence throughout his life and he said, "My parents were not able to teach me a non-violent way of life and so I looked for acceptance and praise—what Dr. Glasser calls love and belonging—in the local gang. My dad had belonged to the same gang. I moved up through the ranks of the gang by being one of the toughest guys and by having no fear of and no regard for others. I only cared about myself. I took what I wanted from those who were weaker. I have spent a lot of time in jails and prison, but I didn't care. Once, when a judge threatened to send me back to jail, I told the judge that I didn't care and that I still wouldn't obey his orders. The judge realized that the threat of jail was meaningless and he changed the order to something I was willing to do, go to these classes."

Lute said, "Before my last arrest I was doing and selling drugs and robbing others to take what I wanted. I was violent and fought with others just for the sake of showing my fellow gang members, my 'homies,' that I was tough and fearless."

The gang unit of the local police station had Lute's picture placed on their wall, as the leader of the gang and the detectives knew him very well—on a first name basis.

Lute said, "The police had followed me and tried to capture me, but I dodged them and I made fools of them. They couldn't catch me."

Lute has tattoos on his shaved head and on his chest and arms. The tattoo on his throat is a dashed line; under it are the words "CUT HERE." In group, he has related many stories about his participation in illegal activities and the multiple moves he made to stay ahead of the police. He does this with a proud attitude and a smile in an attempt, I think, to impress me and the other group members.

Lute described an argument he had with his wife. "I got into an argument with Terri because I was selling drugs. The police saw the fight but didn't stop it because they wanted to get me for a major strike offense so they could put me in prison for my third strike—twenty-five years."

Terri's version is quite a bit different. "The argument was because I wanted to leave him—and I still do want to divorce him. He backed me into a corner and I stabbed him and hit him in the jaw with my closed fist to get away. He hit me back. The police weren't there and didn't see the fight. I left home and reported the domestic violence to the police."

Lute continued the story of his arrest. "Terri left the home and the police approached the house. There were several of my homies in the house when the police came and I decided to give up and start a new life. I told my homies to go before the police could arrest them and I stayed in the house so that the police would find me and take me to jail."

Terri reports, "Lute's story sounds courageous of him, to let his homies go, but it was eight o'clock in the morning and only family was present—

an uncle and little cousins. The police had the house surrounded so no one could have left."

Lute said, "I hid in the closet and when the police searched the house, they found me. Several of the cops knew that I was going to go quietly, but the one cop who actually found me tried to act tough. When the cop came at me and tried to take me down, I broke his nose. The other cops just watched. I gave up when they closed in on me. All the while, I was seeing the vision of my daughter taking her first steps. I left with the police without more fighting."

Terri said, "Lute argued with the cops and told them to 'F' off. He was taken out in handcuffs."

Lute said to the group, "I wanted to be a part of my daughter's life, watch her grow up, and take many more steps because I still have the vision of her first steps in my mind."

Terri responded to Lute's desire: "Lute had seen his daughter walk many times before the arrest, but he was usually high and he doesn't remember any of her real first steps."

Lute reported to the class that he was charged with intimidating a police officer and the court ordered him to jail for one year, to do clean-up on the California highways, and to go to fifty-two domestic violence classes.

Lute said, "I refused to do the clean-up and got additional jail time instead. I took the domestic violence classes, and I didn't press charges against my wife and so she wasn't charged with anything. It was a mutual combat case and I only responded to her attack."

Terri said, "Lute was charged with the domestic violence charges. He threatened me into dropping the charges and I lied to the district attorney. I told the D.A. that the bruises were from wrestling with dogs at my work as a veterinary technician. The D.A. wanted to charge me with making a false report, but decided against it."

Lute said, "I was in and out of jail in a fraction of the year due to an overcrowded jail condition, and I started the domestic violence classes here. I'm not required to do alcohol or drug counseling."

Terri said, "Lute was out of jail in two days."

Lute reported in the group, "I don't want to be away from my daughter, son, and wife any more. I want us to live without hassle. My ideal life changed from one of gang leader to one of more love and belonging with self power instead of external control and power. What I was doing before would not change my life into what I wanted. I decided to come to the group as ordered by the judge and gain all of the information I could in order to bring peace into my life."

Lute claims, "I have taken full responsibility for the abusive behavior toward my wife."

Yet, when Terri's point of view is considered, we see that this statement may not be fully truthful.

Lute's son by a different drug-addicted woman was living with him and Terri before the domestic violence incident and continued living with them until there was an incident in a bar.

Lute said, "Terri and I were having a social drink and I was playing pool. It was hot in the bar and I took off my outer shirt to get cool. The tattoos showed from around my undershirt and some of the other men in the bar recognized the gang tattoos and started to give me a hard time. I told Terri to leave the bar and that I would take care of the situation. Terri was frightened and left the bar. I took care of the situation without resorting to violence and left the bar."

Terri said, "Lute, I, and one of Lute's friends who had a blind date, went to a pool hall and bar. The blind date was from a foreign country and spoke little English. Lute didn't take off the shirt in the bar and we played pool until the bar closed."

Terri said that she believes Lute doesn't consider what can happen to the people with him when he takes off his shirt. "He takes off his shirt to purposely show his tattoos when there are men around because he thinks that his wife may be looking at them. He is like a peacock, showing his feathers and impressing others. In this case, he is trying to impress them on how tough he is and his gang affiliation."

Terri reports, "Instead of being in the bar, we were getting into his friend's SUV outside of the bar and some men from the bar were waiting outside in their Suburban. Lute was too drunk to realize that the men were pulling up to the SUV at a high rate of speed. The next thing I heard was one of the guys in the Suburban telling the driver, 'No, fool, don't do it!' I turned my head to see what was going to happen and pulled on Lute to tell him that the men were about to do something. The Suburban sped past us and left without further incident. Instead of being worried for the safety of all of the people, Lute started yelling at me and said, 'Why are you staring at them? Do you see something that you like?'

"We all got into the SUV and started to drive home. Lute cursed at me and called me a whore. His friend had to turn up the radio to drown Lute out because his blind date was asking questions about what was going on between Lute and me. I was crying because of these accusations and the way Lute was talking to me. These actions hurt me very much.

"When we got home, I decided that I couldn't continue living with him because I am afraid for myself and my children. This was only one of many times he had put us in danger because of his gangster mentality and his abusive words."

Lute has said in group, "I do not blame, degrade, or commit acts that dehumanize my wife. I do not want to put her safety at risk."

Terri reported, "We decided to move into a hotel and Lute took all of the furniture and possessions and put them in storage. All of those things belonged to me from before we married, but he wanted to control them. Lute wanted me to give up my job and just stay home and take care of the children, but since the hotel was $500 more expensive than the house had been, I had to continue working.

"There was another aggressive incident that occurred when I was trying to drop off our daughter at the babysitter's home. Lute was angry and stood in the car doorway so that I couldn't close the door and back out of the driveway to go to work. I asked him to move many times and he refused and stood his ground. I finally got out of the car, pushed, and hit him to get him to move. Lute countered by punching me with his closed fists as if he were in a boxing fight. He finally moved out of the way and I was able to leave."

Lute told the group, "I moved out of the house and found another home in which my son and I could live. My son and I started with little or no furniture, but I was able to furnish the home after a while—one piece at a time as I could pay for it—first a bed for my son and some cooking items, then a TV, couch, chair and a bed for myself were added one at a time."

Terri said, "We were living in the hotel and after the fight Lute and his son moved in with his grandmother. Lute left his son in my home with his daughter and me. He didn't move into an apartment until later. When Lute finally moved into an apartment, his son joined him. The other two children and I moved into a confidential residence for safety."

Lute went to court to gain full custody of his son because, he said, "My son's mother was using drugs and was neglecting him."

Terri had worked as a legal aid and she helped Lute organize his papers so that he could present a case against his son's mother. Lute was awarded full custody of his son as a result of his attendance and participation in the group, reporting that he was staying clean and sober, holding a steady job, and not being in trouble with law enforcement. His son's mother continues to lead a life of drug addiction and tries to gain custody of their son. According to Lute, the court favors the mother by giving her multiple chances to make changes even though she continues to fail. This is consistent with the prevalent philosophy in the United States court system of trying to keep the mother and child together at all costs.

Terri told me, "At the court hearing, Lute sat next to me, in front of the bailiff. He put his arm around me and told me that if I mentioned or pressed charges for the domestic violence, he would have me killed. Lute doesn't spend much time with his son and has his grandmother baby-sit the boy much of the time. Even when Lute is with his son, his son watches TV in his room while Lute is in the other room reading or doing his own thing. He is not a good father to his son."

Lute's daughter continues to live with Terri as Lute and Terri still have separate residences. Terri continues to see Lute when she brings their child for visitation. Terri has another child by her first boyfriend. That man can only have monitored visitation with his child due to sexual abuse allegations. That man allegedly touched his daughter in a sexual manner. Children's court has forbidden Lute from being around this stepchild because of his violent past.

Lute has told the group that he has had many trying events while living alone. "I have had three cars with my tools in them stolen by my mother. Because of my record, I have not been able to gain much assistance from the police to recover the cars or prosecute the thief. I even found one of the cars in my mother's yard, but the cops wouldn't arrest her."

Terri believes, "Lute is the product of an unfaithful and an angry mother. Lute never got to see his father. His mother never told him who his father was. Lute discovered the identity of his father later in life."

Lute reports, "I have faced my father and decided not to have a relationship with him due to our past fights. He was a gang member before me. I was able to do this without resorting to violence or excessive anger. I have not made threats to harm to my father in any manner in solving this problem."

Terri says, "That's a lie, he has threatened his father by saying, 'Let's go outside.'"

Lute stated in group, "I have realized that the changes in my behavior were not well enough established to rely upon to overcome the anger and resentment that I feel for the past abuses and neglect—especially if I visit his home. I am afraid that I might get into a fight with my father and so I just stay away from him at this time. I do allow my father to visit with my son once in a while."

"I only want my children to be proud of me and my newly chosen life."

Lute is an active learner in the group and demonstrates his intelligence and leadership qualities.

Lute was the foreman of a construction crew and had taken responsibility for the work of the crew and relationships with the customers. He reported, "I quit my job as foremen at the work site because I didn't want to take the harassment from my boss. I quit the job during an argument with my boss and am waiting for him to apologize to me before I will return to work."

"I started going to school to learn a back-up trade in the medical field in case the construction work cannot support me or if I become physically unable to continue the work."

Terri said, "He dropped out before completing the classes."

Lute responded, "I dropped out of class because I couldn't keep up the payments."

It is very easy to see how he became the leader of his gang because he is a leader in the group. He has learned the elements of the chart that Dr. Glasser generated and reports that he applies its concepts to the events in his life. One of his co-workers confirms that he is a supportive supervisor. Lute reports, "My behavior illustrates the choices I have made. I use the actions in my relationships with my family and customers that don't push them away from me. But I admit that I still don't have much compassion for other people in my life."

Lute has determined the level of his basic needs and now reports making choices that will satisfy the needs and bring him happiness.

So far, Lute reports, "I have been violence-free since coming to the group. This includes all forms of violence including violence outside of my marriage, too. I believe that eventually Terri and I will be able to live together again when I am off probation and have demonstrated the changes I am making to her satisfaction. I understand that the use of coercion or violent behavior to maintain dominance is unacceptable in an intimate relationship."

Terri reports, "Lute continues to use drugs some of the time and I still live in another town away from him. I have resigned my job and am living on welfare. Lute pays child support as long as I continue to see him. I believe that Lute would stop the child support if I leave him completely. He tries to maintain the relationship by giving me some money for child support. Lute moves from one job to another so that the courts can not catch up with him for scheduled payments of child support."

Terri reports, "Lute is still very possessive and jealous of me and wants to know who I'm talking with, what I'm doing, and who my friends are. This is oppressive and I don't want to live with him because of his control of my relationships with friends. Lute is able to deal with greater and larger frustrations and disappointments, but I am still afraid that he will lose control of his anger and get violent again when Lute sees something as serious or when he is under the influence of drugs and can't control himself. I am considering divorcing Lute and ending the relationship completely, but I continue to help Lute retain custody of his son and prepare court papers for Lute when he has to go to court to defend his full custody with no visitation ruling."

This behavior of Terri's gave mixed signals to Lute and he stated that he hopes that they will get back together someday. Lute continued to use coercion with Terri in the form of rewarding her with child support to control her and keep her from leaving him.

Lute's attendance in group became sporadic and inconsistent and he fell behind in his payments to the agency so the agency had to drop him from the class. His initial commitment to change faded and even though he gained the knowledge of how to bring peace and calmness into his life, he was unable to follow through with the necessary changes.

The information presented in this book is straightforward and makes sense to those who read it, but the implementation of the principles requires a constant effort and may be very difficult. Lute was trying to overcome many years of learned behavior and that takes time and a continued commitment. He and Terri have divorced and he has lost custody of his son to the maternal grandmother. He is required to have monitored visits with his daughter, if and when he decides to visit with her.

APPENDIX B

Example of Community Response
to Aggression, Jeremy's Story

This appendix tells of a youth who has been denied his happiness by his parents and the community. Suggestions as to what the community can do to provide the opportunity of mental health for all people are given in Chapter Three, *Community's Role in Happiness.* You may know of many children such as Jeremy who have been led into a life of unhappiness by the unfortunate limitations of a society that believes that external control and punishment is the proper manner to teach our youth how to be healthy and happy.

Jeremy's Story

Jeremy is a ten year old boy who has violent outbursts in class and at home. The signs of his temper frighten the children and teachers in the class and the adults around him at home. He throws things, drags other children across the playground, and has been suspended on five occasions. He is passing all of his classes, but the school is very concerned about his violent behavior. He was suspended one time because he refused to participate in an art activity. Instead, he used scissors to cut paper and then engaged in the totally inappropriate behavior of throwing the scissors on the floor. He refused to give the staff the scissors, threatened and was disrespectful toward the teacher. He intimidated the teacher and instigated a classmate to join in his acting out. Another time Jeremy hit a student on the bus and threatened to stab an adult. He cursed the adult and "gave him the finger," then refused to follow directions from the principal. A third suspension came when he started to misbehave in the bus at the end of the school day. He showed his middle finger to a classmate and then insulted another student. He made a big mess on the bus and the bus driver could not leave because of the acting out behavior. When a teacher tried to calm him down, he called her retarded and used the "F" word. His mother finally was able to calm him down.

The school system uses suspension as punishment when the child is too disruptive to the rest of the class. This is excessive discipline in many cases and may be just what the child wants—to get away from the control of authorities and school. Instead of using the caring habits, the school system uses the deadly habits—and as a result, the child moves away from education and societal integration and toward the isolation and uneducated total behavior that often leads to a life of crime.

Jeremy attends a special school for students with anger, aggression, and discipline problems. This school has specially trained teachers who are capable of attempting to educate students that act out emotionally, disturb the regular classrooms, and distract the teacher and other children from learning in the traditional manner. He had been assigned to this school because, at his regular school, he had been angry with a female student, grabbed her and dragged her across the playground, causing injuries to her legs. He had also verbally threatened teachers and had been so angry that school staff had to restrain him forcefully. His teacher has recommended that Jeremy be placed in a facility where his violent behavior can be corrected.

Neither of his parents, Martha and Henry, nor the school could control Jeremy by using external control so they wanted assistance in putting him in a residential educational setting. They believed that he could receive behavioral modification training from professionals on a full-time basis in such a setting. At least that is the superficial reason that they gave. The fundamental reason is that since no one could control Jeremy—not the parents, the school system, or the mental health workers—they believed they needed to put him away from the rest of society. This is one of the more common methods of dealing with children who do not conform to the standards of conventional educational institutions. In other words, if they will not respond to external control and the deadly habits, and then keep them away from those who will. Most educators would support on-campus alternatives that teach, but there is no funding, so the next best choice for the safety of others is to place the child elsewhere.

Jeremy is in both individual and family counseling. He is also in a group for anger management. No one is teaching Jeremy to choose to stop the aggression when he does not get his way, or teaching the adults in his family how to deal with his aggression without external control and in a caring (Choice Theory) manner.

Jeremy's mother had been using cocaine prior to his conception, but stopped when she found out that she was pregnant. She started using again when he was one year old. Jeremy's mother and father divorced when he was eighteen months old due to the physical aggression against his mother by his father. At six, Jeremy and his father moved away from his mother to a different state. While he was in the custody of his father, his father whipped him with a belt, hit him with his hands, and generally tried to control him with force and physical punishment. When Jeremy reached seven, he became too large for his father to control forcefully. His father gave custody of Jeremy back to his mother to finish the job of raising him. Martha had been an addict and alcoholic for the first seven years of his life and was actively sober for the next three years. She, too, lacked the parenting skills to deal with Jeremy's acting out. She resorted to loud arguments and some physical punishments, too. She lacked the patience and knowledge of how to deal with a demanding child like Jeremy without trying to overpower him and force him to do as she wished.

Both of Jeremy's parents lack the education and information on parenting to be effective parents for a child who responds to external control and power parenting with aggression and hostility. Parents who understand and use Choice Theory are better suited to deal with this type of difficult child. Jeremy's grandparents did not have the knowledge or did not feel the need for these parenting skills, and the social system does not have a method of teaching these skills to parents before the need becomes apparent and society has to intervene forcefully in the lives of the family members.

Henry returned to the town in which Jeremy and his mother lived. He moved close to Jeremy so that he could have visitation and then return him to his mother when he started acting out. Henry continues to use the belt and hits Jeremy when the child does not do what Henry commands.

The social workers from Children's Services have been called to Jeremy's home on many occasions. The first time was when Jeremy was four years old. At that time, he was involved in an emotional abuse investigation due to his mother's drug use and the domestic violence in the family. The next year the emotional abuse investigations involved his father and a physical abuse investigation involved both parents. When he was six, a sexual abuse allegation that could not be substantiated was filed against his mother. And finally, there were emotional abuse, general neglect, and physical abuse allegations that involved his sister and his mother as perpetrators. Children's Services took no action that could improve the parenting skills of Martha or Henry so that the children could have a life free of excessive discipline and harsh punishment.

Jeremy came to the attention of the Department of Children and Family Services again because of the physical punishment that Henry and Henry's girlfriend, Donna, inflicted upon him.

Jeremy had been playing table games with Donna and her grand-children when one of the other children brought the family's pet bird into the room.

Jeremy said to the other child, "Take it out of the room. I don't like the bird."

Donna responded by saying, "You don't have to take it back to its cage."

When Jeremy sighed very loudly and rolled his eyes, Donna got very angry and said, "Don't be disrespectful to me."

As Jeremy tried to get up and walk away, Donna pushed him back down on the bed. This set of actions was repeated two times with both parties getting even angrier with each other. When Donna came at Jeremy a fourth time, he thought she was going to hit him so he put up his foot to stop her, kicking her in the stomach.

Later during the investigation, Donna reported that she thought Jeremy had kicked her, not that he was defending himself from her attack. Her perception of the event was that Jeremy had kicked her as part of the fight and Jeremy's perception of the event was that he was defending himself from her attack. Both are accurate, but truth is in the mind of the perceiver and not in the event itself. The event was that Donna's stomach came in contact with Jeremy's foot. All of us act on the events in our lives, as we perceive them and not on the reality of the event. Disrespect is in the eye of the beholder. We match what we think that we see and hear with what we think we should see and hear. When they do not match, we totally behave to bring the two in synchronization. We attach meaning to the actions of others and totally behave based on our interpretation of the meaning. Often we do not bother to ask why someone acted the way he or she did. We just react to our interpretation.

Donna said to her grandchildren, "Go get the belt. I'm going to teach Jeremy not to disrespect me." She yelled at Jeremy, "You are disrespecting me. Don't do it any more. I'll teach you not to disrespect me."

When her grandchildren returned with the belt, she took it and spanked him about three or four times on his bottom.

An older child of Donna's came into the bedroom and said, "If you touch my mother again, I'll hurt you."

Donna got up and left Jeremy on the bed crying.

Soon after, Henry returned home and, after Donna told him her version of what had happened, he spanked Jeremy again. Jeremy called his mother to take him home. When Martha came, they talked and she decided to leave her son with Henry. She told Jeremy to behave himself and apologize for his disrespectful behavior to Donna.

After his mother left, Jeremy said, "I'm going to bang my head against the wall until you let me go home with my mother."

When he noticed that neither Henry nor Donna was paying any attention, Jeremy stopped making the threat.

Later Jeremy said to his father, "I want you to move away from Donna and live in your own apartment because I don't like Donna and she is the cause of all of the arguments." It was in this way that Jeremy was asking for his need for love and belonging to be met by his father.

Based on this incident, the local law enforcement establishment concluded that this was not a child abuse. They classified the event as a domestic argument that evolved into a physical confrontation due to Jeremy's anger management problem. However, due to the past history described by the adults in Jeremy's life, officials decided to bring the Department of Children and Family Services into contact with the family.

When I went to the home to visit with Jeremy and his mother as a Children's Social Worker, I found Jeremy home alone.

I asked him why he was home alone and he explained, "I was suspended from school for acting out and my mother had to go to work."

I called his mother. "Martha, it is not appropriate to leave your son at home alone and you need to come home to take care of him."

Martha responded, "I have to be at work or I'll get fired. I can't take any more time off. Jeremy's acting out at school has used up all of my sick leave."

I said, "If you can't come home or have someone come to take care of him, I'll have to take him into custody to provide him with the safety that he needs."

Martha said, "I'll call my mother. Can you wait until she comes over to the house? It will be just a few minutes."

I said, "I'll wait and I'll make sure that he is safe until his grandmother arrives."

Jeremy's grandmother arrived in a few minutes and agreed to take care of Jeremy until Martha came home from work.

Martha invited me to attend a meeting at school with the Department of Mental Health to initiate an evaluation of Jeremy so that he could receive more extensive special education and possibly a residential placement. When Jeremy went to the University of California-Los Angeles Neuropsychiatric Institute (UCLA-NPI) for treatment, he had been diagnosed with Obsessive-Compulsive Disorder. His current psychiatrist diagnosed Bipolar Disorder. The Diagnostic and Statistics Manual of Mental Disorders, 4th ed. (DSM-IV), defines Obsessive-Compulsive Disorder (OCD) as follows:

> The essential features of Obsessive-Compulsive Disorder are recurrent obsessions or compulsions that are severe enough to be time consuming or cause marked distress or significant impairment. At some point during the course of the disorder, the person has recognized that the obsessions or compulsions are excessive or unreasonable. This recognition does not apply to children because they may lack sufficient cognitive insight into the reasonableness of the obsessions or compulsions. The obsessions or compulsions must cause marked distress, be time consuming, or significantly interfere with the individual's normal

routine, occupational functioning, or usual social activities or relationships with others.

The DSM-IV goes on to state that the there is a specifier, "With Poor Insight."

This specifier can be applied when, for most of the time during the current episode, the individual does not recognize that the obsessions or compulsions are excessive or unreasonable.

Note that, with this exclusion and specifier, almost every child qualifies as having this disorder at one time or another. Examples would include learning to play a video game or having a girl or boyfriend. The perception of a child's behavior by adults creates a totally different view of reality than that of the child. The perceived world of the child is very different from the perceived world of the adult. The child does not have all of the tools in his behavioral system to achieve his needs. Mature adults have many more tools in their behavioral systems to deal with life's frustrations. The total behavior that the child chooses to use to satisfy his needs comes from a significantly reduced behavioral system than that of the mature adults and may seem to be out of reality to an adult. So, the adult labels the immature child as OCD. This is a matter of perception on the adult's part.

Bipolar II Disorder is often characterized by episodes of mania alternating with episodes of depression, or mood swings that are not caused by recognizable events. The DSM-IV definition has many sub-characteristics and qualifications, but the general public does not know these sub-characteristics and qualifications and their implications. These lay people may be quick to "diagnose" this disorder for the convenience of labeling and categorizing the person. This categorizing allows them to view such an up-and-down behavior as bipolar so they may dismiss any search for the underlying need that the sufferer is trying to meet.

The lifetime prevalence of Bipolar I Disorder in community samples has varied from 0.4 percent to 1.6 percent, according to the DSM-IV, but many more children wear this label than the percentages would indicate. The major depressive, manic, mixed, and hypomanic episodes must be distinguished from episodes of a mood disorder due to a general medical condition. The symptoms must cause clinically significant distress or impairment in social, occupational, or other important areas of functioning. Individuals with Bipolar II Disorder may not view the hypomanic episodes as pathological, although others may be troubled by the individual's erratic behavior. The above distinctions are seldom considered when the diagnosing is performed by non-therapeutic people. In Jeremy's case, a psychiatrist made the diagnosis, but it was based on lay persons' observations reported to him instead of on his own observations of Jeremy. In contrast, the diagnosis of Obsessive-Compulsive Disorder from UCLA-NPI was based on actual observation of the patient by the diagnosing psychiatrist.

The purpose of the meeting at the school was to discuss the history of the family and the activities of his parents in raising him. As we were getting ready for the meeting, one of the licensed therapists from the Department of Mental Health said to me, "The only reason that we are letting you into this meeting is because mother invited you here. These meetings are confidential and we can't give the information out to anyone. Even school personnel aren't allowed to sit in on these evaluations."

During the course of our discussion, Jeremy became aware that we were at the school and started acting out in his classroom. He had taken a test and done poorly on it. When the teacher asked him to correct the mistakes, Jeremy had wadded up the paper and refused to make the corrections. The teacher asked if we could have Jeremy in the meeting so that she could eliminate Jeremy's disruptive behavior from the classroom. The committee agreed to have him in the meeting room and to let him draw to keep him busy while they continued with their assessment information gathering. When Jeremy came to the room, he was seated at the table with the committee and soon became a part of the assessment. Jeremy was able to provide much information as to which parent had done what to him and when they had done it. He is an excellent historian of his life's experiences.

About a week later, I visited his home to meet with his half-sister and to make a second evaluation of his safety in the home setting. I interviewed his half-sister, his maternal grandmother, Martha, and finally, Jeremy. His half-sister, mother, and grandmother had described an incident that took place two days prior.

Martha said, "Jeremy got angry because he wanted to go to one of my (twelve step) meetings with me and I told him that I wanted to go by myself. When I take Jeremy with me, I can't concentrate on my recovery and I have to make sure that he is entertained so he won't disrupt the meeting. Jeremy got mad started throwing things in the house."

I asked, "Did he hit you?"

Martha said, "No, if he hits me he knows that I will call the police and have him arrested for battery. He'll go to juvenile hall."

I asked Martha, "Did he break anything?"

She responded, "No, Jeremy knows that if he did, it would be vandalism and I would call the police and have him arrested and taken to juvenile hall." She continued, "Jeremy is careful not to cross the line that would get him placed in jail. Jeremy has at times pushed me when he is angry and has threatened teachers at school, but he doesn't hit any adult. The school suspends him and the police won't take him for just pushing me. So, I'm stuck with him. That's why I want him in placement."

Jeremy had been taking medication for his anger management, but recently Martha felt that the medication was no longer working so she stopped giving it to him.

She said, "Jeremy refuses to do anything I ask of him and he becomes angry when I insist. I think that if Jeremy were to live in a residential facility that provides twenty-four hour supervision along with mental health services, he could learn how to control his temper."

Jeremy was able to behave in an acceptable manner while I was talking with the other members of the family. When I finally got to Jeremy for his interview, we went into a separate room so that we would not be overheard by others.

I asked Jeremy, "What about the outbreak two days earlier?"

Jeremy admitted, "I got angry because I couldn't attend the meeting with Mom."

I said, "You chose to behave properly at the meeting at school and you chose to behave properly while I was interviewing the other family members today."

Jeremy nodded in agreement and then I asked, "Why did you choose to act out when your mother told you that you could not attend the meeting with her?"

He thought for a while and then I asked, "You did *choose* to act out against your mother, didn't you?"

Jeremy gave me an impish grin that indicated I had uncovered his secret and that the answer to my question was yes, he had chosen to act out so that he could get his way.

I asked Jeremy, "Like they say in your mom's meetings, I just pulled your covers, didn't I?"

Jeremy smiled and nodded again. He said, "I bring on a lot of my punishment with my attitude and my anger with Mom and my teachers."

I said to him, "It is your choice, isn't it?"

Jeremy said, "Yes."

If I had asked him why he makes the choices he makes, Jeremy would not have been able to answer the question, but an outside observer can answer it. Jeremy is trying to build a life with only one tool—anger. It is like a contractor trying to build a house by only using a hammer. If

Jeremy were taught more tools to meet his needs, then he could have more choices of which tool to use. He would not be so disruptive in school and with his family. But this approach requires the people who come in contact with Jeremy—the community—to help teach him these tools and to support him when he tries to use them.

A few weeks later, a case manager in the Department of Mental Health told me that they had decided to place Jeremy in a residential facility for full-time treatment. Martha had agreed to the placement and the department was looking at facilities out of state. Jeremy would be sent to a facility that was thousands of miles from his home and family.

This incident illustrates the difficulty that our current systems of care have with parents and children who are not *normal* or *average* or willing to act within the confining parameters of the school system, mental health system, parenting system, social services system, the health care system, and the criminal justice system, not to mention the clergy system, the media system, and the governmental system. The community, state, and nation as a whole are not equipped to provide adequate services to raise a child like Jeremy to be a productive citizen. He will be pushed and prodded by the elements of society until he lands in one institution or another so that society does not have to deal with him daily on a face-to-face basis. This young man could, with the introduction of self-worth and Choice Theory, be shown how to make more appropriate choices so as to have meaningful relationships in his life. He could learn to be a happy, productive member of society. It is a shame that without major changes in the manner in which children such as Jeremy are treated by the community, they will be lost to society and may even be a large financial drain on the community, state, and nation.

Jeremy is typical of many children in the American society today. His story describes how the community sees and deals with these children's attempts to be happy and enjoy life. It is clear to me that the community's approach to solving what it has labeled as Jeremy's mental health problem is, in many cases, counter-productive. The execution of a more productive approach is not practical in society as it is currently organized, but maybe in the future we will be able to address the problems of families like Jeremy's in a more coordinated and effective manner. The use of punishment to get people to do what we want them to do is not effective. The large number of repeat offenders in jail is proof that punishment without education does not change people. Dr. Glasser and those who advocate the use of Choice Theory suggest that its use in our homes, schools, and communities would create major improvements in the mental health and well-being of the people there.

Jeremy is being denied his mental health by the current system of health and behavior control systems in his society. *Family aggression and domestic violence are public health problems.* Leadership roles are given to the people in the general population, clergy, media, social service providers, the educational system, the justice system, the government, employers, and the health care system itself. The concept of community involvement and responsiveness to the issue of family aggression has been advocated by many leaders. Community opinion strongly states that aggression is unacceptable. This leads all of our social institutions to expect full accountability from the aggressor, but the only tool we have now is to apply consequences and external control to those who violate the agreed upon laws and rules.

Aggression is a learned behavior that starts in childhood. If it goes unchecked or if the aggressor achieves his or her desired outcome from the behavior, it will continue into adulthood. The adult aggressor is subjected to criminal courts action, but it is the childhood aggressor that is exposed to many of the elements of the community as it attempts to modify the learned behavior. For the community to be successful, it must act in a coordinated manner with the sole objective to help the child learn alternate total behaviors to deal with frustrating situations.

Partial Annotated Bibliography

Dr. Glasser created annotated bibliographies in Appendix C of *Every Student Can Succeed* (2004) and on the William Glasser Institute Web site (www.wglasser.com) of the following books and it is included here to assist the reader in understanding the purpose of each of the books. This is not a complete annotated bibliography of all of the books that are referenced in *Happiness in the Family*, but does include some of the more often referenced books used in developing the concepts discussed in the text.

For Parents and Teenagers: Dissolving the Barrier between You and Your Teen. In this book, Dr. Glasser asks parents to reject the common sense that tells them to lay down the law and ground teens, or coerce them into changing their behavior. Instead, he offers a Choice Theory approach and suggests that the teenager's behavior is more likely to be in harmony with the parents' wishes when there are fewer efforts to exert control.

Warning: Psychiatry Can Be Hazardous To Your Mental Health. This is the first major book to focus on mental health, rather than mental illness. Dr. Glasser discusses the hazards of being diagnosed as mentally ill; being treated for a non existent illness, often with harmful brain drugs; and, worst of all, being told there is nothing you can do for yourself. In this book, you will learn that you can, in fact, do a lot for yourself.

Counseling with Choice Theory, the New Reality Therapy, formerly titled *Reality Therapy in Action.* This book is the expanded, clarified, updated version of Reality Therapy. Dr. Glasser invites the reader to sit with him while he counsels a variety of clients and reveals the explicit core of his counseling method, sharing his thoughts as the counseling proceeds.

Choice Theory, A New Psychology of Personal Freedom. This book is the basic theory for all Dr. Glasser's work. Choice Theory is a non-controlling psychology that gives us the freedom to sustain the relationships that lead to healthy, productive lives.

Getting Together and Staying Together. Dr. Glasser joins with his wife, Carleen, to examine the question of why some marriages work and others fail. The Glassers advise readers how to create loving and happy relationships by applying Choice Theory.

The Language of Choice Theory. This book gives special examples of how to use Choice Theory language in parenting, marriage, school, and work; it includes imagined typical conversations in real-life situations comparing controlling or threatening responses with those using choice theory.

Choice Theory in the Classroom. This book translates Choice Theory into a productive, classroom model of team learning with emphasis on satisfaction and excitement.

The Quality School, Managing Students without Coercion. This book develops the concept of a Quality School where there is no failure because all students are doing competent work and many are doing quality work.

Every Student Can Succeed. This is the most useful book for teachers. It takes teachers to a new level of excellence and demonstrates what to do and say to reach challenging students. By the end of the first year, school can be a joyful, connecting place in which all students will learn and many more will gain competence.

Reality Therapy for the 21st Century. This book gives immediately useable skills and techniques highlighting lead management and cross-cultural applications, and answers questions about research supporting the effectiveness of quality schools.

References

Abrahams, Nadine; Casey, Kathleen; and Daro, Deborah. 1989. *Teachers Confront Child Abuse: A National Survey of Teachers' Knowledge, Attitudes, and Beliefs.* Chicago: National Committee to Prevent Child Abuse, working paper no. 846, p. 10.

Alberti, R. and Emmons, M.1974. *Your Perfect Right.* San Louis Obispo, CA: Impact.

American Humane Association. 1994. *Child protection leader: Domestic violence and child abuse.* Englewood: American Humane Association.

American Psychiatric Association. 1994. *Diagnostic and Statistical Manual of Mental Disorders, Fourth Edition,* Washington, DC: American Psychiatric Association.

Berkowitz, L. 1970. Experimental investigations of hostility catharsis. *Journal of Consulting and Clinical Psychology*, 35, 1-7.

Boffey, D. B. 1997. *Reinventing Yourself: A Control Theory Approach to Becoming the Person You Want To Be.* Chapel Hill: New View publications.

Brown, Resa Steindel. *The Call to Brilliance.* Thousand Oaks, CA: Fredric Press.

Collins, Simon, (2006). APN Holdings NZ Ltd, Feb. 14, 2006.

Daniszewski, J. Feb. 6, 2006. Column One, *Los Angeles Times.*

DiMassa, C. M. Dec. 24, 2005. Falling Through the Cracks, *Los Angeles Times.*

Ellis, A. 1979. Rational-emotive therapy. In: Corsini, R. (Ed.), *Current Psychotherapies* (pp.185-229). Itasca, IL: Peacock Publishers.

Ellis, A., and Harper, R.A. 1975. *A New Guide to Rational Living*. North Hollywood, CA: Wilshire Books.

Gibbons, J. and de B. Katzenbach, N. Commission Co-chairs. 2006. *Confronting Confinement: A Report of the Commission on Safety and Abuse in America's Prisons*. Vera Institute of Justice

Glasser, William. 1984. *Control* Theory: A New Explanation of How We Control Our Lives*. New York: Harper & Row. *[The word "Control" has been changed to "Choice in later publications."]

Glasser, William. 1994. *The Control* Theory Manager*. New York: HarperCollins Publishers Inc.

Glasser, William.1998. *Choice Theory, A New Psychology Of Personal Freedom*. New York: HarperCollins Publishers Inc.

Glasser, William. 1998. *The Quality School: Managing Students Without Coercion*. New York: HarperCollins Publishers Inc.

Glasser, William; Glasser, Carleen. 1999. *The Language of Choice Theory*. New York: HarperCollins Publishers Inc.

Glasser, William. 2000. *Reality Therapy in Action* [or in paperback, *Counseling with Choice Theory*]. New York: HarperCollins Publishers Inc.

Glasser, M.D., William. 2000. Glasser, Carleen, *Getting Together and Staying Together*. New York: HarperCollins Publishers Inc.

Glasser, M.D., William. 2000. *Chart Talk*. Chatsworth, CA: The William Glasser Institute.

Glasser, M.D., William. 2001. *Choice Theory in the Classroom*. New York: HarperCollins Publishers Inc.

Glasser, M.D., William. 2002. *Unhappy Teenagers, A Way for Parents and Teachers to Reach Them* [or in paperback (2003)] *For Parents and Teenagers, Dissolving the Barrier Between You and Your Teen*. New York: HarperCollins Publishers Inc.

Glasser, M.D., William. 2003. *Warning: Psychiatry Can Be Hazardous To Your Mental Health.* New York: HarperCollins Publishers Inc.

Glasser, M.D., William. 2004. *Every Student Can Succeed.* Chatsworth, CA: The William Glasser Institute.

Glasser, M.D., William. 2005. *Defining Mental Health as a Public Health Problem.* Chatsworth, CA: The William Glasser Institute.

Greenfield, L. 1998. *Alcohol and Crime: An Analysis of National Data on the Prevalence of Alcohol Involvement in Crime.* U.S. Department of Justice, Office of Justice Programs, Bureau of Justice Statistics Report # NCJ-168632.

Kaufman-Kantor, G. and Asdigian, N. 1997a. When women are under the influence: does drinking or drug abuse by women provoke beatings by men? In: Galanter, M., ed. Recent Developments in Alcoholism, Volume 13: Alcoholism and Violence. New York: Plenum Press, Pp.315-336.

Kaufman-Kantor, G. and Asdigian, N. 1997b. Gender differences in alcohol related spousal aggression. In: Wilsnack, R and Wilsnack, S., eds. Gender and Alcohol: Individual and Social Perspectives. New Brunswick, NJ: Rutgers Center of Alcohol Studies, Pp.312-334.

Leonard, K. E. 1993. In: *Alcohol and Interpersonal Violence: Fostering Multidisciplinary Perspectives.* Martin, S. E. ed. National Institute on Alcohol Abuse and Alcoholism (NIAAA) Research Monograph No. 24. National Institutes of Health (NIH) publication No. 93-3496. Bethesda, MD: The Institute. Pp. 253-280.

Lopez, S. December 11, 2005.. *Mentally Ill in the Jail? It's a Crime.* Los Angeles Times.

Morris, Steve and Jill. 2003. *Leadership Simple, Leading People to Lead Themselves.* Santa Barbara, CA: Imporex International, Inc.

Murray, E. 1985. Coping and anger. In: Field, T., McCabe, P., and Schneiderman, N. (Eds.), Stress and Coping (pp. 243-261). Hillsdale, NJ: Erlbaum.

NCCAN, *1990 Summary Data Component.* Washington, DC: Dept. of Health and Human Services, *April,* Working Paper No. 1), 1992.

Primason, Richard. 2004. *Choice Parenting. A more connecting, less controlling way to manage any child behavior problem.* New York, iUniverse, Inc.

Ranchor, R. 1995. An evaluation of the first step PASSAGES domestic violence program. Journal of Reality Therapy, 14(2), 29-36.

Reilly PM and Shopshire MS. 2002. *Anger Management for Substance Abuse and Mental Health Clients: A Cognitive Behavioral Therapy Manual.* DHHS Pub. No. (SMA) 05-4008. Rockville, MD: Center for Substance Abuse Treatment, Substance Abuse and Mental Health Services Administration, reprinted 2003 and 2005.

Stets, J. and Straus, M. 1990. Gender differences in reporting marital violence and its medical and psychological consequences. In: Strau, M. and Gelles, R. eds. Physical Violence in American Families: Risk Factors and Adaptations to Violence in 8,145 Families. New Brunswick, NJ: Transactions Publishers, Pp.151-165.

Straus, M.; Gelles, R.; and Steinmetz, S. 1980. *Behind Closed Doors: Violence in the American Family.* Garden City, NY: Doubleday.

U. S. Department of Justice. April 1998. *Alcohol and Crime.*

Westat, Inc. 1998. Study of National Incidence and Prevalence of Child Abuse and Neglect: 1988. Washington, DC: U.S. Government Printing Office. pp. 5-24.

Wills, D. 1995. *The Criminal Justice Response: Domestic Violence.* Los Angeles, CS: Publication of the District Attorney's Office.

Wubbolding, Robert E. 2000. *Reality Therapy for the 21st Century.* Philadelphia, PA. Brunner-Routledge.

Yellen, Andrew G. 2004. *The Art of Perfect Parenting and Other Absurd Ideas.* Northridge, CA: Yellen & Associates.

Warren, J. June 8, 2006. *High Cost of Prisons Not Paying Off, Report Finds.* Los Angeles Times.

978-0-595-43129-8
0-595-43129-1